Love Lives On

*A Personal Insight into
Understanding and Coping
with Grief*

THERESA MOLONEY

Published 2012 by
Veritas Publications
7–8 Lower Abbey Street
Dublin 1
Ireland
publications@veritas.ie
www.veritas.ie

ISBN 978 1 84730 359 2

A catalogue record for this book is available from the British Library.

Designed by Dara O'Connor, Veritas
Printed in Ireland by Gemini International, Dublin

Veritas books are printed on paper made from the wood pulp of managed forests. For every tree felled, at least one tree is planted, thereby renewing natural resources.

This work is dedicated to my husband, Brian, whose gentle, caring love guided me through the pain; to the memory of my parents, Margaret and Paddy, whose love sustains me to this day; and to my beautiful son, Harry, through whom my parents' love lives on.

Contents

PREFACE

Just after midnight on an otherwise unremarkable night in January, my mother's heart slowed and eventually stopped beating following a short illness that prevented her from reaching her sixty-fourth birthday. Eleven days earlier, unknown to my mother, my father died of the very same illness.

These words set the context for this beautiful book by Theresa Moloney, who allows us to accompany her on her personal odyssey through the territory of grief. To do so is a privilege, because Theresa permits the reader personal access to each element of the grieving process in all its inevitable manifestations, its contradictions, its revelations, its progress, its raw profundity and personal pain.

Grief should not be visited upon the young, and what makes this book remarkable is that it is written by a woman in her twenties who experienced the death of both her parents, becoming overnight an 'adult orphan', deprived of the support of at least one parent when called upon to suffer the loss of the other. In these circumstances, Theresa had to respond simultaneously to bereavements that were 'poles apart' because, as she herself describes it: her father's death after a number of years suffering from Alzheimer's disease was a 'foregone conclusion', while her mother's death was 'completely unexpected' and something for which she was utterly unprepared.

It is inadequate to say that what happened to Theresa was unfair. To grieve is difficult. To be twice afflicted – to have to respond concurrently to the complexity of two dissimilar grief responses yet under the emotional collective of 'parents' – is exceptionally so. This is one of the elements that makes this book important, because it shows the courage, the resilience, the support of faith and the wisdom that can emerge in those who are young. How much we can learn from them when they are given the opportunity to articulate, in their own words, their own experiences of living this life.

The death of Theresa's parents precipitated her into grief without its usual supports: without the prop of time, the shield of experience, the balm of parental presence or even the personal comprehension of her peers. In our twenties, life should be free, filled with hope, suffused with promise and unencumbered by grief. Instead Theresa was submerged in grief's process, encountering the shock, disbelief, undeniability, sadness, loneliness and coldness of death's finality.

Life is often mysterious but never more so than when we are called upon to respond to death, for it is then that we encounter that most profound, pure human emotion that is grief for those we love. We discover that death does not end love but brings it into sharp focus and transposes it into a new and immutable state.

There is no right way to cope with grief, as Theresa herself recognises. However, there are many ways that can damage the bereaved if they seek anaesthetisation through substances, addictions, avoidance or artificial means of circumventing the realities of loss. Theresa did not try to dull her pain; instead she had the courage to enter into it, to scrutinise and analyse it, to document it and eventually to gift others with her observations of loss and its revelations in this beautifully narrated book.

It is the nature of grief that we cannot avoid it, but we can share it and in that sharing comes some healing. The way through grief is to go through it, to enter into it, feel it, describe it, articulate each emotion, provide every detail, narrate each moment of the where, the when, the why and the minutiae of our experience of loss. This is what Theresa does. In *Love Lives On*, she honours her parents, expands her own consciousness and shares her encounter with loss for the benefit of others.

With this generosity, Theresa reveals many of the nuances of grief: the intensity of its surprising physical pain; the distress of sleeplessness; the overpowering shadows of guilt, regret and despair; and the inevitable 'if only' thoughts that torture most people who are bereaved. She identifies the longing, the yearning, the way we cling to the personal belongings of those who are gone, calling upon remembrance with all our senses in order to recapture that which is lost. She recognises how life is divided into 'before and after' bereavement; how life is altered and arrested; how the world stops when someone we love dies and how perceptions of life are changed forever.

I am honoured to have been asked to write the preface to this book, because as a psychologist I know that despite the vast psychological research on the process of mourning, the pain of bereavement and the pathways through grief, there is an inevitable chasm between theory and the lived experience of losing someone we love. Grief is a sacred space: a space each of us must inevitably occupy at some stage, in some way in our own lives. We are also, I believe, called up to accompany others appropriately and compassionately when grief befalls them and when they need our understanding and support.

Grief may have its commonalities, but anyone who has mourned knows that loss is also particular, personal, private and felt in the deepest indescribable recesses of the psyche and the soul. Yet what is most remarkable about grief is that despite the abysses into which we as human beings are plummeted, we can, and we do, emerge again in hope.

Nobody describes this hope as well as Theresa herself when she says:

> You may find one day that you wake to notice the sun streaming through the window and, without realising, you become caught up in its beauty. You'll get lost in a beautiful melody and, for the briefest of moments, your pain won't be the centre of your existence. You'll laugh a little more and cry a little less. A day will come when the memories will make you happy instead of sad. And you will have come to realise that somehow, unimaginable as it seems, you've managed to carry on.

This is the most important message in this beautiful book.

Marie Murray
Clinical Psychologist

INTRODUCTION

I dreamed of you again last night. You were where you always are when you come to me in these dark lonely nights. You lay on a hospital bed, a man on either side of you. On your left, the man you loved, lived for and gave your heart to. On your right, a complete stranger. Your eyes found me first. They glistened with joy. That crooked smile — the result of an illness you overcame but that you hated so much — lit up your face beautifully, despite what you might have thought. Your hands came into focus. Your left held your husband's hand and he smiled along with you so contentedly, as if you both knew some wonderful secret untold as yet to the rest of the world. The other hand held onto the stranger, so alone but for you. I looked for your eyes once more, puzzled. When our eyes met, I realised that you didn't need to speak; you didn't need to explain. This one simple gesture explained who you are. Your life's work summed up perfectly by this gesture of love.

Just after midnight on an otherwise unremarkable night in January, my mother's heart slowed and eventually stopped beating following a short illness that prevented her from reaching her sixty-fourth birthday. Eleven days earlier, unknown to my mother, my father died of the very same illness. A doctor once told me that in years gone by, pneumonia had often been known as the friend of the dying. In retrospect, I can say pneumonia may have been a friend to my father in his final days. Robbed in many ways of his dignity, bereft of over eight decades of life's memories and experiences, Alzheimer's disease had left him a shell of who he had once been. Unable to eat or drink, perhaps pneumonia had been his friend in ending such suffering. For my mother though, pneumonia was a heartless thief, silently depriving her of a joyful existence. From her family, stealing its very heart and, along with it, the endless and now forever-unknown possibilities for the future.

For the rest of the world a new year had just begun. But I found myself in the strangest of worlds. I was an adult orphan. Two innocent dates in January were now imprinted on my brain forever. Time stopped. Everything was now measured in a before and an after. There is something eerily lonely about losing two parents. Suddenly everything I had come to know ceased to be. Everything had changed in the most fundamental way possible; the foundation of who I was had not only been shaken, but had fallen. At a time when others were planning new beginnings and dreaming of the future, I yearned for the past. But more than that, in those early hours and days after my parents' deaths, I struggled to breathe. I ached for my mother in particular, every moment of the day. A primeval longing pervaded my soul. The physical pain was greater than any pain I had ever experienced. And I truly did not believe that I would survive it.

Perhaps this is where you find yourself today. It may be that tears stream down your face and you don't even notice them anymore. A part of you is missing. Sleep no longer comes and you begin to dread the dark. The silence of night releases the twin demons of guilt and despair. Regret is a constant companion. You cannot bear to look at or touch your loved one's belongings. Or perhaps you carry with you an item of their clothing, breathing in deeply the scent of a lost love. You long for one more year, one more day, one more hour, one more embrace. Your longing is compounded with despair, for you know in your heart of hearts that it will never be.

Grief's pathways are rarely straight. You run downhill, surprised at the speed you have gathered, to suddenly meet a steep incline that, without warning, slows you to a crawl. The road ahead is often unclear; it meanders and at times you find that it doubles back, returning you to where you started. You find forks on the roadway forcing you to make decisions you are unable to bear. The road signposted 'If Only' appears scenic and attractive, but once you follow its course you are led to a dark and dangerous place. Tree-lined roads offer refuge – shade from the sweltering heat of the sun, shelter from the heaviest rains. However, it is but a short-lived respite and however much you long to stay there, you have to leave that refuge and continue along the rocky road of grief.

The innumerable clichés you will undoubtedly be proffered on your journey fail to support in the way in which they were intended. *It will get better. No one knows the mind of God. Time is a great healer. At least they are not suffering now.* At times, given the dark and lonely place in which I resided, they angered me, these clichés. Other times I silently walked away from the people uttering these words. The simple truth is this: there is no way around grief. Platitudes attempting to minimise the inevitable and unavoidable pain rarely achieve their goal, however well intended.

My hope for you is that you will join me on my journey. And that in doing so, you may find a little peace. When you lose a loved one, you are essentially changed forever. You may feel that it will never be better and time will not heal your pain. And while time may not completely heal your pain, you might find the intensity of that pain lessens. You may find one day that you wake to notice the sun streaming through the window and, without realising, you become caught up in its beauty. You'll get lost in a beautiful melody and, for the briefest of moments, your pain won't be the centre of your existence. You'll laugh a little more and cry a little less. A day will come when the memories will make you happy instead of sad. And you will have come to realise that somehow, unimaginable as it seems, you've managed to carry on.

A lot has been written about the stages of grief. It can sometimes appear as if every person who experiences loss moves from one stage to the next, following a map of sorts. But, unfortunately, there are no maps in grief. Denial and shock, pain and guilt, anger and bargaining, depression and finally acceptance are undoubtedly part of the grieving process and emotions you will feel at different times and in varying intensities. However, it has been my experience that no two people grieve in the same way. As such, this book does not follow these 'typical stages' in a linear way. Instead, emotions and issues are presented as they occurred on my journey, as they have arisen and re-arisen for me, sometimes long after I thought they had been dealt with.

This book seeks to capture the devastating lows and examine the raw emotion that becomes part of life following the loss of someone deeply loved. You may well find that these emotions will strike more powerfully at different stages in your journey than was my experience; perhaps at these times, a specific chapter title will appeal to you in particular. In whatever way and at whatever time these emotions crop up in your own journey through grief, they must be confronted to allow you to take that tentative, often hesitant, first step forward.

This book also provides support as you are faced with the practical realities associated with loss. As I share my experience of my parents' funerals, I hope that it will aid you through this arduous and agonising task. The dying moment, that extraordinary second in time that changes everything forever, is reflected upon so that you too can make some sense of that instant when you lost your loved one and your very existence was shattered. The book explores the burden of painful duties that you would prefer to avoid, the effort of errands you never want to face and the headache of painful responsibilities that you feel unable to perform. I ponder how it is possible that the world can continue on as if nothing has happened, as if it has not been bereft. I suggest ways in which the memories of your loved one may be evoked and treasured. I consider the language of death and particularly how difficult it is to hear your loved one's name associated with the past tense when you are unable to let go. I explore how to cope during times that were so special to you and your loved one; times like Christmas, birthdays and special celebrations which now may well be lonely and painful reminders of what you have lost.

The main thing I have learned on the road of grief is that the company of another who has walked the same road can provide some comfort. I hope that my story will help guide you in your own passage through grief.

THE LONG GOODBYE

I wondered what it was like in your world, in your head, in your thoughts and mixed-up mind. To the stranger, you were a confused old man. Some days you didn't even recognise your family. You forgot names and faces, stories and memories. You were no longer the man we knew. Did you want to talk? Did you have something specific to tell us? Did you wonder why your legs would no longer function as they should? And those days when you were angry, was it your frustration coming to the fore? Did you know that we still loved you? Your eyes were so lost; I missed their sparkle and shine. And I wondered more than anything, when you finally took your leave: did you see things clearly, did the fog lift and did you once again become the man you had been?

As my father was diagnosed with Alzheimer's disease approximately three years before his death, I had a lot of time to ponder some of the deeper issues the illness brought to the fore. The more difficult recurring questions I struggled with were: what is it that makes us who we are? What are we if not a combination of our life's experiences and our memories? Is it not our sorrows and joys, our hopes and dreams, our daily encounters, our everyday routines that make us who we are?

Our body is like a mirror reflecting life's journey: the scar representing a childhood injury; the laughter lines reminiscent of happy, carefree days; the broken fingernail that never again grew straight, the result of a work accident; the injury that serves as a reminder of a sporting triumph; the tattoo that expresses individuality; or greying hair, the colour of life's wisdom. Just as every single body is a map that tells a unique story, the mind is also the manifestation of a life that has been lived. The times we have been loved, praised, hugged, kissed, supported, built up or taken down; the hurt we have experienced, the times we have hurt others. It is all of these experiences that make us the person we are: stored up in our hearts and minds, our past shaping our thoughts and decisions as we look to the future.

This is what I lost as Alzheimer's took hold of my father, imprisoning more and more of him as time went on; shutting me out and locking him in. Communication was so very complicated, if possible at all. So many memories were imprisoned, so many experiences missing. There were black holes where there should have been the light and colour of happy memories. I wondered where he was one winter's afternoon when I sat in front of him and he didn't appear to see me. His eyes, glazed over, wore a faraway expression, and wherever he might have been, I was certain he was not with me. I agonised over it, wondering if he was happy in some memory that he could not communicate to me or if he was simply nowhere, lost in the mist.

There were other days when I could glimpse him just for a fleeting moment before he was gone again. Then there were days when he remembered my name, when he knew who he was, when he could access a memory. It was so difficult. To acknowledge that you can do nothing to 'fix' your loved one is another cruel truth of the disease; all a family member can really do is stand by and watch as a little more of their loved one is lost, day by day. I refused to accept that this was now *who* my father was. Instead I consoled myself with the knowledge that it was simply *how* he was. While the illness attacked his mind, it could not touch his heart, and this was a reality I clung to fiercely. Our minds store memories, while our hearts store emotions, and my father's heart was surely full to the brim with a lifetime of love that could not be taken away.

In the end there was no other way for him. And the fact that I knew this well before it happened meant that the grief associated with my father's death has been somewhat different to that which I had to face in dealing with my mother's passing. The shock was not as great, yet the disbelief was. I knew he was dying and yet when he died I still found it so hard to believe. I struggled with his lack of presence even though it had been fading for years. In body and mind, he had gradually disappeared before my eyes. But now that he was in fact gone, it was utterly incomprehensible for a long time.

It came as a surprise to me that there was a sense of relief at my father's passing: an emotion I did not experience when my mother died. I felt no guilt about this, although I have known many others in similar circumstances who have. One of the more distressing elements of Alzheimer's for me was that a lot of the behaviours associated with the disease become apparent only in retrospect. A lot of my father's strange and sometimes aggressive behaviour before diagnosis could now be accounted for as the early stages of the illness; and following his death, I struggled with the realisation that perhaps I hadn't displayed enough understanding or had not been sufficiently compassionate towards him.

Imagine the following scene. On one side of a lake, there lies a large rock. On the opposite side, there is a pile of stones. In total, the pile of stones equals the size of the large rock. For months and months, very gradually, one stone is taken from the pile and is thrown into the lake, creating a gentle ripple each time as it makes contact with the water. The large rock remains untouched, staying in its place where it always has been. Eventually one day, the final stone is thrown into the lake creating its ultimate ripple. As this happens, without warning the large rock is suddenly hurled into the water with a thunderous splash, causing not ripples but waves to burst forth, disturbing not only the lake but everything surrounding it.

While the grief I faced, and continue to face, regarding my mother and father's deaths is inherently interconnected and irrevocably linked, it has proven for me to be more appropriate to deal with each one separately. In dealing with the death of my parents I have found myself dealing with two experiences that are poles apart, despite the fact they took place so close to one another. My mother's death was completely unexpected and shocking, while my father's death was a depressing, foregone conclusion, and even though I didn't know it at the time, this was something to which I had somehow become reconciled. On reflection, perhaps, as my father's illness progressed and he stopped having an active role in my day-to-day life, my mother had taken on an even greater role as a result. Although we were always very close, my relationship with my mother deepened significantly in the years before she died. As a result, the loss of my mother completely overwhelmed me, but more notably, it devastated my daily life significantly, whereas I had learned to exist without my father's presence in the struggles and triumphs of the everyday.

The stark reality is that what I have lost are my parents. The two people who, together, represent so much: my life-giving source, my beginning, my guides in so many different ways, my allies against the world, my counsellors, my fan club, my future. The significance of two people that for so long felt like one united presence cannot be underestimated. Naturally, therefore, I could not speak of my experience without discussion of the effect of both their deaths. It is, however, the effect of my mother's passing that captures a central role herein, reflecting the central role her love had in my life to the day of her death and, just as significantly, beyond.

How did your loved one die? Were you aware of their impending death? Was there a diagnosis and did you receive a time limit of sorts? Knowing your loved one is dying cannot prepare you for that shattering moment when their last breath leaves their body. It may, in fact, be even harder to accept, as you cannot fully believe that it has finally happened despite many months of discussions with doctors and carers. Your loved one may have discussed their death with you, and difficult though that was, to not hear their voice anymore is derailing. If your loved one suffered and their illness was painful and protracted, you may well have felt a sense of relief, as I did. As a result you may feel uneasy or guilty at having felt this relief. This is a completely natural response, for your mind is in conflict. When you love so much you may well feel relief that that person has finally been freed of their pain, and yet how can you possibly feel relief that they are gone? It is just one example of the complexity of emotions to be confronted.

Or it may have been that your loved one's death was sudden, completely out of the blue, without warning. This kind of death can take a long time to sink in and you may find that your mind will, for a long time, refuse to believe what has happened. You may well feel cheated and struggle with not having had a chance to say goodbye – this can bring its own issues of regret.

The experience of each death is individual. So, as might be expected, the feelings surrounding that death are just as unique. Even within a family dealing with the same death, the emotions of each family member will often be completely different. However the death happened, however you lost your loved one, there simply are no right or wrong feelings. Equally there is no right or wrong response to what you are feeling. In the early moments after your bereavement, do what you need to in order to survive the day. Some may find the only respite is sleep; for others, it may be to express their feelings. Most importantly of all, you must be gentle with yourself.

DISBELIEF

My mother left just as my father had, dying as Tuesday gave way to Wednesday. 'My time is done now, I am finished,' Tuesday said to Wednesday. 'You must carry on now and finish the week.' But Wednesday didn't want to. Wednesday didn't want Tuesday to go. Wednesday was scared. Wednesday didn't feel ready. Tuesday always came before Wednesday, guiding the way. Wednesday wanted Tuesday to stay, to show the way for a little longer. But Tuesday had no say. Tuesday's time was done and Tuesday had to go. Despite Wednesday's protestations, Tuesday said, 'What I have started, I now pass on to you.' And then Tuesday was gone, never to return.

It is some time after midnight on Wednesday, 21 January 2009. Earlier, along with my three brothers, I had attended the removal of my father – that part of the farewell process that brings the finality of it all home. Numbness pervaded the evening and I railed at the unfairness of having to do this now. I was in my twenties and wanted desperately to have been older when I bade farewell to my father. I felt unprepared. I felt like a child, desperately wanting my father to parent me and tell me it would be okay. The strongest memory of the evening was evoked through touch. I remembered as a young child holding my father's huge fleshy hands. I really believed that he must have had the biggest hands in Ireland; surely the hands of a giant. All I had to do was close my eyes and, moving away from the image of death, my hand was in his once more. I could feel it.

That evening was a blur of people, of tears, of words, of the constant repetition of 'sorry for your troubles'. It was an evening of disbelief in so many ways. It was hard to process the many faces who came to be with me on that night. It was a night full of obligation. We stood beside the coffin and every time I looked at my father lying there, I felt a stab to my heart. I felt that it was wrong. Even though it looked like my father was sleeping, I knew it was not so, and that deeper, more pragmatic part of my brain almost taunted that he was not.

As the steady line of sympathisers passed me by, I wondered about it all. I wondered at the words that people used – 'I am sorry for your troubles', 'I'm sorry' – sometimes muttered by those who did not or could not, for some reason, look at me. It was a mystery to me on that night when the most random of thoughts and memories fought for attention. I had no time to reflect on these feelings, as soon afterwards we went back to the hospital – a place that had become an unwelcome home of sorts – to be with my mother.

Just before my mother died, she was unconscious. Her children surrounded her: holding, touching, kissing, crying, laughing and loving as she had done. She must have known; she must have sensed the love and the heartbreak. I have spent countless hours since, wondering, debating, hoping that she did. Such an outpouring of emotions must have penetrated the depth of her unconsciousness. And when that final moment came at the closing of her day, did she look upon us? Did she smile on us proudly? Did she give one final wistful glance, sorry to go, and then move towards her waiting husband?

We left intensive care soon afterwards to be together and to attempt to place some semblance of order on what had just taken place. Looking back now, it was an incredibly bizarre time; and as I remember, I do so in an almost dreamlike way, as if the events that unfolded happened to someone else. I remember burning myself with the hot water the care team provided for tea and coffee. I remember the elderly priest with the kind face. I remember him telling us that in his considerable life experience he had only once come across a similar situation in which two parents had died in such a manner. All of a sudden, time was no longer important. For my mother, time was finished. That is an incredibly difficult concept to comprehend. For so many weeks, I had been tied to my mobile phone and I engaged constantly in time watching, making sure I wasn't away for too long. Now it no longer mattered. There were no phone calls I had to take or make. All that mattered was here, and for me, that night, all that mattered was gone.

We returned shortly to be with her again. She was now freed of the wires and tubes that had encumbered her and that she had endured so bravely. She looked as if she was sleeping. There was the slightest smile on her beautiful face that made me sure that wherever she was, she was in a more peaceful place than where she had been. I took in every single detail of that face. I traced every line. For the briefest of moments, I was happy for her. She had undergone so much suffering in her twenty-eight-day illness, struggling to breathe and in such constant pain and discomfort that, for a time, I was able to appreciate how much she deserved to be free. It did not take long though before the devastation of my new reality struck.

The initial moments following the death of someone close are surreal. If time and perspective are allowed, in retrospect there may be a sense of privilege at having been present for the death. But there was no perspective for me that night, just the deepest sense of loss, sadness and disbelief. I remember how cold the night was. I remember a dark, cold starry night full of ice and frost and I remember how hard it was to breathe.

When I finally got home, at about two in the morning, I was no longer the same person. Now – when I needed them most – my parents were gone.

The practicalities of the next day took over for a short while. One of the more painful aspects of that night was amending a poem I had written for my father's Funeral Mass, now for my mother's Mass. She was not, and now never would be, told of his death. I wanted her to know that I would have held her, that there was no need for her to go too. I wouldn't have asked her not to be sad. I wouldn't have told her not to cry. I would have been there. I spent an hour before going to bed doing what needed to be done. Sleep did not come easily, and when it did, I awoke often, hearing an imaginary phone ringing. When you dread the worst and the worst happens, the body tends to go into a protection mode of sorts, and in those first few hours – as I have done countless times since – I wondered if it was all a dream. It was in this haze that I existed in the days that followed.

To say that it is hard to come to terms with such a loss is one of the greatest understatements that could be made. In the early hours and days of disbelief it is impossible to accept that the person who is the cornerstone of your life is no longer there: the parent who has been a part of your life forever; the spouse who shared your children, your home, your world; the child whose life you would have gladly swapped for your own; the friend and constant companion who knew all there is to know about you. Your disbelief inhibits you from understanding that there are conversations that will no longer be had, that there are moments no longer to be shared. Disbelief, though, is your body's way of protecting itself; there is so much that needs to sink in, that were you to understand the enormity of it all at the beginning of your journey, you may not cope. It is completely normal and natural but it is an incredibly difficult emotion to deal with as it can worsen the pain. Your mind fails to comprehend what has happened and yet proof is absolutely everywhere. Acceptance of your new reality is perhaps unthinkable at this stage, yet it will come.

The First Farewell

It was, without question, the most surreal moment of my life. To walk into the church – in which we have sat together, gossiped perhaps a little too much, and shared a lifetime of Sundays – without you was like walking into a shell of a building. Worse than that, you, who had carried us all, now had to be carried. It was a dark day and one I had never even contemplated. I was struck by how utterly wrong the situation was. I struggled with a goodbye that I never wanted to utter.

My mother's Funeral Mass was a poignant yet beautiful experience. It was a comfort to me on that grey, lonely day that belonged to winter, and it is still a comfort to me now. It brought me some solace amidst devastation. My mother's funeral took place just three days after my father's. When there was light and hope, we had made the decision as a family to delay my father's funeral. In doing so, we'd hoped my mother would be well enough to be told of his death. Sadly, it was not to be. My wish then was that, taking place so soon after my father's, it would be individual and relevant to her. I wanted my mother's to be as different to my father's funeral as they were as different to each other in life. Otherwise, I would have felt that I was doing her a disservice. I strived to create something that was special, different and appropriate to her, which is the best tribute I could pay.

The funeral involved a Catholic removal and Mass. It took place in the parish church in which my mother had played a big part. She lived a stone's throw away. The church bell resonated daily within the walls of her home. From her front door, she could glimpse the church's cross rising over the evergreen hedge. For years she had cleaned the very church in which she now lay;

polished the tabernacle door until it shone, and gently, lovingly tended the flowers and plants. She had sung in this church. She had prayed here to God, in whom she trusted completely. She had, reluctantly at first, believing herself to be unworthy, distributed Holy Communion at Sunday Mass. She had been at the centre of the parish, living out her life to the best of her ability and giving of herself. It was appropriate that it was here that I would say my first official goodbye.

Flowers lined the steps on the way in: a perfect tribute to my mother who took great pleasure in nature, whose house was filled with plants she nurtured and talked to every day, whose garden reflected every season. The flowers she cultivated and loved often graced the altar beside which her coffin now lay. Two photos of her were placed in the church. One was a picture of her together with the husband to whom she had dedicated herself. The second was a photo of her laughing with a clown, expressing perfectly her love of life and sense of fun.

I spent some time choosing the most suitable readings and, in the end, I settled on a reading from the Book of Ruth (1:16-17) because it echoed my mother's giving of herself to her family. It spoke of 'your people being my people', reflecting how my mother had loved and cared for my father's family, becoming a part of them and making them her own. It spoke of 'dying where you die'. It was fitting in the most poignant way possible. The Gospel reflected my despair and my desperate hope that there is some kind of afterlife and that my mother does live on. I choose the story of the death of Jesus. A number of significant people in my mother's life offered up prayers of the faithful, and as they did so, I offered up my own desperate plea that wherever she was, she could hear them.

One of the more beautiful elements of the Funeral Mass was when a number of women who had worked with my mother in the parish church for many years came at offertory time to dress the altar. Carefully spreading out the white altar cloth, laying candles on the table, bringing the bread and wine and, finally, gently placing my mother's Eucharistic Medal – they added their own love and sorrow to the Mass. It was deeply upsetting to look upon my mother's friends in the heartbreaking knowledge that she would never again be part of their group. And, as it would so many times afterwards, the injustice of the whole situation struck me hard.

At the Funeral Mass, people had an opportunity to receive the host and also to receive from the chalice. This was important to me because my mother, as a Eucharistic Minister, would have appreciated the gesture, which is ordinarily reserved for special occasions.

As the coffin waited to be incensed and I waited to speak, I worried that I would be unable to do so. I had fallen too far into the depths of despair. The gentle wafting of incense caught my senses; I breathed the smell in deeply and was reminded of childhood days. I reached out and touched the wisps of incense just as the sun shone through the window, illuminating the darkened church. In that moment, I felt comforted and strengthened and knew then that I would be able to speak.

The strange thing was that, as my mother left the church for the very last time, I searched for her. My three brothers were carrying her coffin and, for an instant, I felt totally alone. I was jarred by how anomalous this was. I remember turning my head to see where she was. Every time my mind denied reality, the shock of the truth eventually returned, taking with it my breath. The church bell rang out, leaving a bitter, lonely echo in its wake, marking the end.

I have always been fascinated by liturgy. The ritual and symbol involved seem to reach out at a subconscious level to caress our senses, resulting in an experience that speaks to a deep part of who we are. By our very nature we are ritualistic, our daily lives made up of so much ritual and symbol, in which we readily partake, perhaps without reflecting on it at all.

Our earliest memories involve many rituals. A child participates in the simple ritual of a birthday celebration, aware that the cake is coming, watching as the candles are lit and secretly rejoicing in the knowledge that they are the only one permitted to blow them out. We store up memories of a Christmas rich with symbol. There is the gathering of family, many of whom will make long journeys to be part of this important assembly. There is the use of the many associated signs and symbols, including the robin redbreast, the Christmas tree, the snowman, the holly. Weddings are full of ritual and symbol also – the white dress, the giving away, the exchange of rings, the declaration of vows witnessed by family and friends. We live our lives through ritual and symbol, so it is quite appropriate that they play a part when the time comes to bid farewell.

Participation in liturgy, including the Funeral Mass, seems to mirror the many rituals and symbols at play in our secular lives. Perhaps that is why it is comforting to us. If we can participate in it at such an upsetting time, a sense of the sacred can be sparked. This sense of the sacred is something which transcends what we know and it can bring a vestige of consolation.

The familiarity of the farewell ritual may draw you in. It will offer you an opportunity to cry. You can cry openly and speak genuinely of your shock, disbelief and utter despair. In the days, weeks and months that follow you will look back and quite possibly be amazed at how you got through the day itself. So much of it is the ritual carrying you through. You speak the well-known words. You perform the familiar actions. You have done it so many times before. But this is different. As you utter those words and as you perform the actions, if you are able do so, consciously think about what it is you are saying and doing.

Often, when someone you love has died, you are struggling with the most simple of daily tasks, such as getting up, dressing or eating, and so planning a funeral seems like an insurmountable task. If you simply do not have the energy or will to do it, you might hand it over to someone you trust. But, if you can, try to get involved. Get all the help you can if it will allow you to participate in the process to some degree. Being part of the planning of the farewell for your loved one helps for a number of reasons. Firstly, when your world has spiralled out of control, taking part allows you to take some control back, however little. Secondly, and most importantly, you are the person who knew your loved one the best and therefore you can plan the most fitting farewell. Take your guidance from the one who will preside over the funeral and work within their guidelines, but remember that no priest, minister or officiator knows your loved one as you do. They may have a sense of your loved one, but it is only someone who has loved that person deeply who can truly understand.

To describe your loved one's funeral as a celebration seems like a contradiction. But it can be: try to make it as individual as you can. It is a time to remember, to celebrate the gift of your loved one's life. It is, without a shadow of a doubt, difficult to do so when all you can think about is how you want that life to have been longer, to have gone on. Openly share those real emotions you feel. Don't be strong for anyone. This, the first time you say your goodbye, is about others supporting you.

THE HUMDRUM REALITIES OF LOSS

The building was old. It was cold and I did not want to be there. In fact, it was the very last place I wanted to be. I took a seat on the unforgiving, hard plastic. As I did so I gazed at the shiny red floor and the hideous peach-painted walls, and I longed for my mother.

I have had the happy experience of registering a birth. Now that I consider it, it was a time of the utmost joy. To announce to the world that this special little person, this part of me, has made their debut, has entered the world. This special person who is mine. It was not possible for me to do so without looking to the future and considering the adventures, the life to be lived and shared. At the time of my parents' deaths, I never knew that a death also has to be registered, although on reflection I suppose it makes sense. It is cruel timing that so many practicalities associated with the end of the life must be tended to just as the reality of the loss dawns. Most can only be done by you, the next of kin, nearest, dearest, loved one. I learnt that a death certificate is necessary for many of the practicalities that have to be taken care of.

The learning curve for me was steep, harsh and painful. A few weeks after my mother's death, I rang the hospital to get the medical records so I could register her death. The woman in the medical records office explained that she had no details of my mother's death but … I didn't hear a single word more. Instead this hope inside me leapt forth. Maybe she didn't die at all. I mean, there is no record of it. Then the truly awful reality: *but you were at the funeral.* And here yet again was the reoccurrence of a disbelief that just refused to surrender.

The Registry of Deaths is in fact for births, deaths and marriages. On entering the building, I pulled a ticket to secure my place in a queue to say that, yes, my parents are dead – even though I didn't truly believe it myself. I sat and waited my turn. Just as you cannot but look forward when registering a birth, you cannot but look back on registering a death.

Two lives had ended just like that, without warning, and now officially they were at an end with no fanfare, no nod to their greatest achievements in life. With a simple pen stroke, their deaths became official. I shouldn't have gone there on my own. I'm not sure what I was expecting. But something, some place more sombre, reflective, caring. It should not be in garish office full of excited young couples about to start their lives together or full of babies letting the world know in strong voice that they are finally here, while I sat in confused silence quietly whispering to the world that my parents had died. I wanted it to be a place of warmth, empathy and compassion. While I shouldn't have gone there alone, I wanted to be the one who did it. It had to be me.

There are countless and varied tasks following a bereavement. Some you may accomplish in an almost robotic fashion, doing what needs to be done without really thinking about what it is you are actually doing. You will remember very little, as though you were on autopilot throughout. Others will stop you in your tracks completely and bring your grief to a new level as your altered reality sinks in. Often you will feel that you don't have the energy or strength for all these necessary but now unimportant tasks.

There are accounts to be cancelled, requiring you to admit to strangers that your loved one is no longer here, no longer part of this world, no longer in need of its utilities. You are asked why you need to cancel, and as you utter the treacherous words, once more your heart breaks. It took me a full year to change my mother's phone number on my mobile phone. My brother started using her phone and even though the rational side of me knew it was him calling or texting, I could not let go of seeing her name flash up on my screen before answering. It was a brief but beautiful illusion.

Other matters to be tended to include dealing with your loved one's belongings. It leads you everywhere, this one. Each piece of clothing will remind you of different occasions, each with a story of its own. Every book, piece of jewellery, personal possession that had so much meaning for your loved one is a precious jewel in their story. How can you possibly give anything away? If these belongings were important enough to them to keep, how then can you discard them? You may want to hold on to every single piece of your loved one's existence, of their history, as if to prove that, yes, they did indeed live. And maybe if you keep their possessions, they live on. When the time was right, I let go of a lot of these and held on to the more precious ones. You might do this with someone present or without, whatever feels right to you.

The language used when a will is read is so legalistic, final and cold – devoid of emotion at such an emotional time. It was hard to hear it without imagining my parents, perhaps in the same office in which I now sat, coming there together to prepare this will. And what thoughts, I wonder, were in their heads? Was it simply a matter on a to-do list to be dealt with, or was it more? Did they consider their actual deaths? Did they wonder what ages their children would be upon hearing it read? Did they wonder how we would cope? Were they able, unlike so many people, to truly imagine a world of which they were no longer part?

Organising and printing memoriam cards is another challenging task to be completed in the first year or so following your loved one's passing. There is more work than you may have thought involved. Decisions need to be made on what photo to use and which words should be chosen to best capture your loved one.

In ways perhaps, these tasks help. For a while they can give you a focus, something to do. In the doing, you may feel a short-term release from dealing with the emotion and you may well feel like you are doing something for your loved one. In other ways, though, these particular tasks associated with the end of your loved one's life can be extremely difficult and painful to accomplish. A lot of people may have opinions on when you should do certain things. Make sure that you are ready. It is vital that you only attempt these things then and not before. Don't feel guilty if you need help and are simply not able to face certain responsibilities. For some, a lot of these tasks may take months, for others, years. Some people view them as part of the healing process. For others, it is a part of the terrible grief. Whatever decision you make regarding these practicalities, in carrying them out, do so with a certain degree of caution and try not to expect too much of yourself. This can be a very emotionally draining time. Be kind to yourself.

REGRET

If only … I could have… I wish … I should have … Why didn't I …
If I could do it again … If I had one more day … I lay awake restless
and fearful. The terrible torturous guilt and regret returned worse than ever.
And I knew that tonight would be another night when the darkness would
keep me company.

Together regret and guilt left me completely powerless, because regretting action or non-action is no good. Now that my mother is gone, it is over and I cannot change any of it. Feelings I thought I might have dealt with continued to haunt me, again and again. If we love deeply, we are indeed taking a huge risk.

Regret and guilt can be so difficult to get past when we lose someone. But it is a natural response. I can remember reading about these two terrible emotions for the first time in a leaflet on bereavement a couple of days after my parents died and gasping; my heart stopping for a brief moment as I read exactly what I was feeling. Now, at least theoretically, I knew that it existed in the realms of the 'normal' on the heartbreaking path of grief. This realisation brought comfort only for a fleeting moment. In those early days and weeks, I did not voice my regret and guilt. Instead I thought about it, scrutinising every detail as it engulfed me.

Regret and guilt are so closely linked that it can be incredibly difficult to distinguish one from the other. They are extraordinarily complicated emotions to work through. This is made more complex because they can, unfortunately, go hand in hand. However, defining them can in fact help to overcome them. Accepted wisdom differentiates them thus – guilt is the result of an action that we carry out, knowing at the time that it is wrong, whereas regret is more concerned with an action that, only on reflection, we come to realise may have been wrong. This can be so incredibly liberating if we stop to consider it for a moment: I have come to realise that the emotion I am struggling with is regret and not guilt.

This may relate to the time of your loved one's passing or it may be about other times in their life when perhaps you regret not spending more time with them or telling them just how loved they were. You may regret something you said or did. This can result in reliving that thing over and over. Perhaps as you do so, you change the story so that you no longer regret your actions. But eventually when you return to the present, the painful truth of your regrets is still there. It is these regrets that can lead to feelings of blame and responsibility for whatever it is that you did or did not do.

I had no regrets about the time I spent with my mother. We could not have been closer if we tried. We spent time with each other at least once a day, if not more often; we called each other at least once a day if not more often. In the year before she died we had been away on two holidays together. Our relationship went beyond mother–daughter and dwelled in the realms of very deep friendship. It shifted and moved effortlessly from the trivial and inconsequential to the serious and the critical. It was characterised by a sharing of every facet of our lives. She was my confidant. I was positive then and am positive now that she knew how much I loved her.

Yet I had deep, painful regrets about her illness and how my action or non-action could have made a difference. This regret led to terrible sleepless nights, hours of pain, countless tears and has probably been one of the hardest aspects of my grief. I wondered how someone absolves themselves, lets go. If I got a white balloon and watched it hover and gently take off into the air, if I didn't let it out of my sight until it became a blob of white in an otherwise perfect blue sky, would it take my guilt with it? If I plant a sapling and watch it grow into a strong mature tree, will this torment lessen as it grows? If I pick a beautiful yellow rose and throw it into a raging river, will the river in all its majesty and power take with it my pain? If I plant the prettiest flowers at the graveside and cry enough, will I be cleansed of these awful feelings? Will it get carried away on the wind some day? What is to be done? If I can no longer shoulder it, will it leave me? Would I ever be free?

About eight months after my mother's death, I finally realised where my regrets had led and how connected these feelings were to the whole grieving process and, in fact, why I could not move on from it. It all came to a head one evening as I sat in a theatre listening to a beautiful yet sorrowful singer. The emotion of the song touched me and I noticed that my face was drenched wet from tears. The voice was poignant, haunting yet inherently beautiful. I cried, allowing my tears to fall unchecked in the darkened theatre. I cried for my lost loved one. I cried because she could not share this anymore. I cried because the music perfectly reflected her – beautiful but so desperately sad because she had left and was no longer with me. Exploring my mother's departure became the huge turning point for me in dealing with regret.

It was that night I realised that my biggest regret of all was that I did not make my mother better. Doctor or not, I was her daughter and I wanted to make her better. I held her hand, rubbed her head, gently washed her face and wished with all the love in my heart for her to be better. But it was not enough. I realised that for a strange few months, I wondered if I could have loved her enough to make her better. And there was the heart of my regret. And possibly my answer to the question was, did my mother love me enough to stay alive? Regret can skew common sense, reasoning and logic. Of course I loved my mother enough to make her better and of course she loved me enough to make herself better. Unfortunately that is not how life works. Once I finally grasped this to some level, I was able to work towards lessening the regret and guilt.

One thing is certain, I have come to realise that if I do nothing, only allow myself to feel, then the terrible agony will never go away on its own. It will lie dormant, destined to return when I least expect it. I have found one of the most effective strategies to deal with this is to voice the regret. Find someone supportive who will listen. It may be a partner, a friend, someone who is on the very same road as you, or even a stranger – possibly in the form of a grief counsellor. Take your regret as far as you possibly can. Take your 'if onlys' for a walk and don't stop until they are fully explored. Exhaust your 'I should haves'. Remember that you are looking at all of this in retrospect and that while the outcomes of the tough decisions you made are now crystal clear, you couldn't possibly have known them at the time. Two people helped me in this. One was a counsellor who simply said to me, 'you are not a doctor'. The effect of these words was profound. I remember being unable to stop crying upon hearing them. I remember thinking, 'she's right, I am not a doctor'. And while I know it's a common reaction to blame doctors for not being able to save a loved one, I never experienced this. Instead I blamed myself. So when I heard this coming from someone else, it seemed to lift a weight from me. Another person, a friend, asked me to imagine what my mother would have said to me given everything that had happened. And I know beyond a shadow of a doubt that she would have looked at me exasperatedly, berated me for being silly and told me that she knew I did my best. I know that she would have been heartbroken for me and the decisions I had to make. I know she would not have forgiven me because, in her eyes, there would not have been anything to forgive.

Take the power out of regret. Voice your regrets out loud. Tell other people. By being open about these feelings with others, I've been amazed by the number of people who have felt the same way and by the manner of their regrets. For some it was regretting not having spent enough time with the person, it was a fight they had before the person died, it was not telling their loved one that they did, in fact, love them. In fact, if you look back over your life and relationship with the person, it is very likely that they knew how much they were loved. For others, it was regret that they had some hand in the cause of the death itself. A father proudly buys his son his first car and weeks later the Gardaí call to his house to tell him the unimaginable has happened and his son has been killed in a car crash; a wife surprises her hardworking husband with a week's holiday and, on that holiday, tragedy strikes as he drowns in an unpredictable sea. For others it was a similar story to mine: not taking their loved one to hospital on time, not making the doctors do more, not insisting.

Expressing your regret aloud is very important in dealing with it because regret may well cause you to lose perspective. This may be the only way that you can take the monster that is regret and make it a natural part of grieving. Forgiveness plays a huge part too. Know that you did your best and that your loved one would never want you to agonise over the course of their death. Forgive yourself. Some days you may still need to voice your regret and, once again, in doing so you take the pain and power away from it. And it no longer stabs at your heart.

I Can't Hear You Anymore

You came to me again just before the light of a new day. 'I thought you died,' I whispered, incredulously, hardly daring to hope. 'No,' you said, contentedly, 'not really. I mean my heart stopped, but only for a few seconds. I'm back now. I'm okay.' I couldn't believe it. I took you in my arms gingerly, as though you were a wisp of smoke about to disappear before my eyes. I held you. Afraid to hold on too tight but afraid to let go, I caressed you so gently.

I awakened to the now familiar heartache as realisation slowly dawned. Was it not all a dream? These past few months? I waited for relief to flood my body as it does when you awake, glad to know that whatever terrible dream you were having was, after all, *only* a dream. But the relief never came. Sometimes I wished I could live in that moment, that fleeting second upon waking in the half-light, just before reality devastates a new day. But my mind knew. No dream could last this long surely. It felt as if only moments had passed since sleep finally found me. It was still dark outside. Dawn had not yet broken.

Suddenly, crippling fear descended upon me. I couldn't hear her voice anymore. I thought and thought and tried and tried but I couldn't hear her. I said my name over and over in my head as if she were calling me, as she had a million times before. But nothing. It was not the same. It was not her voice. I wanted, childlike, to reach out and touch her. I wanted to touch her face, to gently trace her features and listen as she spoke to me once more. I wanted to be held by her. The silence of the dark rang in my ears as I longed for her. All I wanted was to hear her voice calming and reassuring me. The pain of missing her was agonising.

I searched frantically for comfort in memories; my memories of her, the ones we made together. But they blurred and jumbled together so that I couldn't recognise a single one. I couldn't remember her. I was forgetting and it was only a couple of months since she breathed. I slept fitfully and woke feeling drowsy and tired and sick. The lashing rain outside had stolen all the light of day. It was miserable and grey and it mirrored my soul. I didn't think I could withstand this. It felt like I couldn't breathe and I thought I was drowning in my pain. It was as if it would never go away, as if it would never change. It would always be the same. Always missing, always in pain, always wondering, always regretting. Do you know what I worried about most? What will it be like when I have lived and missed her longer than I have known her? It is twenty-nine years away but this day was an illogical, depressing sort of day and this is what I worried about.

I had existed through a week of this deep depression when I decided to do something about it. I dragged myself into town in search of an attractive and colourful notebook. I knew I would know it when I saw it. And I did. It was covered in flowers. Over the next two years, this is where I placed my treasured memories of her. Memories struck at all times and in all kinds of situations. I was in the car and as I drove along I noticed the vibrancy of the autumn leaves as they transformed into purples, plums, browns, reds and yellows and I was reminded of her. I was at work and a four year old told me how much she loves her mammy and my mother's smiling face was in my head, and there it is – another wonderful petal on the flower of memory. Other times I thought of my mother and nothing would come. Sometimes it was merely a single word that would spark off so many memories. Often it was when I was out gardening, something we loved to do together.

Or it could be a piece of music or a sunny day and I am overcome with beautiful memories of her.

I am a lover of words. I admire their intricacies. To me, words are conjurers; magicians evoking a thousand images in my head. For my mother, words were significant also. Not eloquent, carefully phrased prose, but rather down-to-earth words that connected her to others. She had so many friends and there were so many conversations. Often she was not exactly where she should have been because she was lost in the moment talking, chatting, reaching out. But during my mother's last days, she could not speak and had to write. She wrote with pencil because it was easier. 'I'll write a book,' she wrote one particularly frustrating day, but her smile was present too. We laughed at the notion.

As I engaged with my memories and used words to capture them, there were two places in particular where I went to be especially inspired. Places where I felt the warmth and comfort of a blanket of memories. Throughout my life I had gone to these places to soothe my soul. The first place was the sea: Kilkee in County Clare, my childhood holiday haunt, a place rich in family memories. I went there one winter's day when the enraged sea matched my mood perfectly. The cliffs, ravaged by years of beatings from the waves, reflected the anger in my soul. The wind howled and the sea raged and I walked and walked. With each step a new memory unfolded itself. The revelation of the memories to the backdrop of the music of the ocean soothed my anger, if not my pain.

The other place was Glenstal Abbey in County Limerick, a monastic community that I had first visited in my late teens. The most noteworthy thing about Glenstal, and what is immediately apparent on arrival there, is the Benedictine welcome that is extended to all. I found this when I returned there following my bereavements. Even though I felt drawn here, I had put off going for a long time, mainly because I found it extremely difficult to meet people who did not know my story. A strange experience for me was meeting someone six months on who did not know what had happened. To find myself telling that story again at that stage was difficult and quite bizarre. It felt as if I was telling a tale I had read, not one I had lived, and it appeared as if the things that had happened to me had in fact happened to someone else and I was merely recounting their story. The more time that passed since my mother's death, the harder it was to tell of her passing to those who had not heard my devastating news. However, when I got there, I was greeted graciously as always, and welcomed with the offer of a listening ear. I told my story once again.

Glenstal's appeal to my senses helped that day too. After I had talked as much as I could, I was welcomed to share lunch – which thankfully for me was held in silence. The psychedelic design on the ceiling of the church captured my attention as I became lost in its pattern and colour. Incense-filled air reminded me of the funerals. The organ-filled church and chanting monks gave me a prayerful and relaxing space. The monastic settlement lies in nature at its most alive and beautiful. And that day it conspired to give me some peace to allow me to indulge in remembering.

Remember your loved one in whatever way is appropriate to you. Perhaps you are artistic. Maybe you draw, maybe you paint. Does colour reach out to you, perfectly reflecting your mood and emotion? Maybe you work with your hands as you mould clay. If so, let your art speak to you and release another cherished memory. It could be that you are a gardener. You plant a memory tree and here is somewhere you go simply to recall those special times. Maybe you plant a bed of flowers in memory. To remember. Perhaps you use sport to let your conscious mind relax and allow your subconscious to be free. When you are running and there are no distractions, your liberated mind can go wherever it chooses. It can, uninterrupted, access your deepest, most cherished memories of your loved one. Maybe you sing or make music. Do it in memory of them. For others it may simply be a good friend who will listen and engage with you as you tell yet another story. Tell that story. Be heard. For there is no greater tribute to a person than that they be remembered. Remember them. Impart the lessons that they taught you and convey the memories of shared adventure. In this way, you will keep them alive in the most authentic way possible.

Every Smell, Every Face, Every Place

I look for you in other people. But, alas, for me you are not there. I turn to nature. I look at the sky and search as the wintry grey gives way to promises of sun. I look for you in the gleaming white of the brand new lily that flowered in my kitchen the day after you died. I search for you in the daffodils as their yellow heads bob in the breeze. I seek your face in the roaring winter ocean. As the waves crash and the foam scatters, I search for you. I search for you in the evening sky as it bids a fond farewell to this day. I search the exquisite orange glow that takes my breath away. I search for you absolutely everywhere. I will never stop.

Once the shock had dissipated, loneliness was ever present. It was a constant uninvited companion that refused to leave. And all you want is to see your loved one again. I would have done absolutely anything to see my parents one last time. Any price would have been worth paying. Longing pervaded my being. It became me. It had been so long and there were so many things I wanted to say. So much had happened in my life that they needed to know. I searched for my mother, in particular, everywhere and did not have to look too hard.

I found her in the garden. She would tell me to use gloves to protect my hands. But I didn't. She didn't either. My hands, often cracked and dry, demonstrated my love of nature just as hers had. The rhododendron in the bottom corner of my garden reminded me of a pleasant Saturday morning we had spent together at a local market buying flowers, and then planting them. The morning had been interspersed with coffee breaks and chats. As my bare hands sifted the slightly frozen earth, I found my mother. As I planted primroses and pansies in their vivacious yellows, oranges, reds, pinks and purples, I saw her shadow. I cried when daffodils and tulips that we planted together announced the arrival of a spring less beautiful because she was no longer part of it. It was in these dark days that I realised it had now been over a year since I'd heard her voice, noticed her smile or felt her touch. I came to the heartbreaking realisation that this life will never be the same again because this longing will exist for as long as I do.

I heard a song on the radio and knew that the last time I'd heard it, she was alive. I went there in my mind's eye and saw her. We were in her kitchen having dinner, as we did so very often together. When I closed my eyes, impeding the present, the aromas of the meal permeated my mind. And as the song ended, she was gone once more. The emptiness hurt and I hated that I always had to come back to the present. It no longer interested me and I was forever haunting the past, the past haunting me – or perhaps we were haunting each other.

I walked the streets of my home town, aimlessly and with no real purpose. I remember looking deep into the eyes of the passers-by. Some met my gaze and then looked away. Others held it for longer than was necessary, perhaps recognising something in me. Their faces reflected my pain. It was only then that I realised. There are people up and down the country in every town and village grieving the loss of a loved one. And I thought it was just me. I searched faces young and old, looking at my own reflection.

There is not a street in Limerick city where she did not tread, and as I walked those same streets, every single one sparked a different memory. The chiming clock on O'Connell Street reminds me of when I was a child and my mother and I would go to an early morning market, full of hustle and bustle and interesting smells. Penney's reminds me of the time we stopped in only to purchase some silly socks, and I can hear her laughter ringing in my ears. Passing a coffee shop, the aroma hits me. All I have to do is close my eyes and we are here together and she is comforting me after what I thought was a failed interview.

Something drew me in to the coffee shop we had frequented so often. I ordered a cappuccino and began daydreaming about our time here together. I was interrupted by the barista. 'To go?' he asked. I didn't reply. 'You want it here or to go?' 'Here,' I said. 'Sure where would I go?' I added half under my breath. He didn't respond. Instead he busied himself with the task of making the finest cappuccino. My eyes, spellbound, followed his every movement. He lifted down a colourless saucer and cup, pouring steaming hot coffee into the white cup, stopping just short of the halfway mark. He frothed the milk with much care. Using a dessertspoon, he protected the precious foam as he poured the milk onto the coffee. When he was ready, he gently spooned the foam on top, before finally sprinkling it with chocolate, thereby completing the perfection. I was lost in the process.

I took a small table by the window. Once, we had sat at that same table. I had stolen the chocolate square that accompanied her coffee. She didn't mind. She never minded. Why did I go there that day when she was gone forever but should have been sitting across the table from me? Maybe I thought that I might find a part of her there. That I might hear her laughter once more. Perhaps I would remember one more story, one more moment that we shared that had long been forgotten. Perhaps. In fact it doesn't matter where I go or who I am with, the reminders are ever present. Some days the memories flood me. They are recent and old, startling and comforting, surprising and upsetting. Some days I feel as if I will drown in all the memories.

The walls of my house are covered with photographs. My fridge is strewn with memories hung with mismatched magnets. They are not posed photos. Instead they are captured moments of a life. I can't remember the last time I looked at those photos, the last time I looked at her face properly, lost myself in her features, looked into her brown eyes that my own so much resemble. All I have been able to manage is a quick glance at her image as I walk past. It has become too painful to linger. I hate the notion of her frozen in time, of her photos ageing. I remember as a child seeing pictures of relations dressed in strange clothes with old fashioned outfits and hairstyles and feeling quite disconnected from them. Instead, I want her to somehow live on and stay alive and relevant.

There came a time when I stopped wishing, stopped letting myself daydream that now she would be sixty-four, sixty-five and healthy. And alive. For so long I thought of all the things we would do. If only. I indulged my fantasy. For a time it helped, just allowing the smallest break from the pain. But reality always awaited me. Now I have come to realise that appealing as it may be, it is not the most helpful thing to do. Still, there are days when my heart will take over, and I will let it and fantasy roam where they want.

People you meet offer countless memories. They give their perspective, which may distort your own. Their stories might come from different parts of your loved one's life, and as they mingle and muddle with your own, you may find that you become overwhelmed by the memories. For they are simply everywhere. There may be days when you feel as if you want to run away and never stop running; to outrun the feelings, the thoughts, the stories going round and round. However, it wouldn't matter how far you ran. If you move away from the familiar – away from the home you shared, the city you lived in, the place you worked – your grief will still be there, as will the memories. You could travel ten thousand miles to the other side of the world, and your grief will be by your side. If you can, make the memories positive. Store them up and be happy for each one that comes to the surface. For these memories can sustain you through the dark days.

WHY ARE THEY LAUGHING?

Two days after my mother died, a refuse collection truck woke me up, and as the cruel reality dawned once more, I looked out the window to see what the noise was. On a cold January morning, the bin men continued to collect rubbish on my street. I watched incredulously as the men grasped the bins' handles, leading them to the awaiting maw of the truck. I listened disbelievingly as the driver reversed his truck right outside my house. This action was accompanied by a piercing tone which hurt my ears. What could they possibly be doing? Did they not know? Leave the rubbish. Let it blow around the streets if it must. Let it be unsightly. Let it pile up and make everywhere an unpleasant, dirty mess. For now in this world so changed it was barely recognisable, it no longer mattered.

One of the long days in the hospital, that are now hazy and confused, regretful muddles, I remember hearing a couple laughing. Strangely enough, the waiting area directly outside the Intensive Care Unit is essentially an open atrium exposed to the sounds below. I remember at first feeling anger at the perceived insensitivity of these people as their laughter rang out, entering my world without first seeking permission. On a day such as this, it would never have been granted. Mine was a changing world; one which was just beginning to fall apart. But most of all, I felt utter confusion. I was bewildered that while my world was crashing down around me, the world of others continued on as if this devastation had never taken place. Not only did their world continue, but it continued in such a way that laughter freely echoed around their world. It was utterly baffling.

Following my parents' deaths, these feelings intensified. Painful as the missing was, in addition to this it was extremely difficult to cope with the fact that life went on. I wanted every sound of laughter to be silenced. The only music that played in my house was the singing of the overworked kettle constantly on the boil. I wanted everyone to whisper, to speak only in hushed tones. The excited, happy conversations had to now come to an end. There was no longer a place in this world for singing and music. Birdsong needed to be muted and the world now should reside in perpetual winter, reflecting my new, cold, harsh reality. Inconceivable as it may sound, if you were happy, I wanted you to hide it. If life was on course for you and your dreams were being fulfilled, then I needed you to stay away. Happiness and joy were no longer welcome in my world.

Amazingly, town still bustled with life. Goods continued to be bought and sold. Buskers still sang as if they did not have a care in the world. I wanted their instruments lowered. I wanted their voices hushed. If they must perform, let their melodies be ones of sorrow and grief. I overheard the music of one of my mother's favourite soaps and automatically thought to record it for her. But then the horrible realisation dawned once more. These characters that entertained her, that she knew so well, would blatantly, insensitively carry on without her. Newscasters continued with their headlines and breaking news stories unaware of the one story that overshadowed them all, the one that completely shattered my world.

I wanted to shout. I wanted to scream out to everyone in this world where life is so precious and so short that, even though they did not know it, their world was not the same place. It had lost two beautiful souls and, as a result, it was distorted, altered forever. This was a fact that had to be recognised before anyone could even contemplate continuing on.

You wonder how the whole world can really not know. You are amazed that the earth is still turning. I'll always remember what my doctor said to me when I met him to discuss my mother's illness a couple of months following her death: 'I don't know how or why, but life goes on.' I was so touched that he qualified it. 'Life goes on' is such a callous statement. When I first heard that phrase following my parents' deaths, a number of angry thoughts came to mind. Life doesn't go on; at least it doesn't go on for me. I was convinced that I didn't want it to go on. I wanted everything to stop, come to a complete standstill and, in doing so, respect what had happened to me. Once upon a time, life and my world existed in a similar sphere. But now that my life and the world were diametrically opposed, I still expected that the world would respect the destruction that has taken place in my life. It didn't and doesn't. My doctor was right. Life does go on. As for the how and why of it? I confess that I don't fully understand that and probably never will. The only way I can think of it is as a new life.

When you lose someone so precious, there exists a new normal and a new reality. Eventually this new life is what goes on. But life as you knew it does not continue on. That life died with your loved one. You may notice that your new life is not as shiny as your old life. The spark has gone. There is a lot of effort required for what used to be the simplest of tasks. Activities and pursuits that once brought you joy are no longer the source of such passion. You may still engage in them but you do so with a heavy heart. Even food and drink that you loved can no longer excite your palate. For a long time you merely exist, going through the motions of days that no longer hold your attention or interest.

There comes a day though when the new reality becomes normal. It is not something that you are conscious of, more something that you will eventually come to a painful awareness of, slowly and over time. It is something you notice only as you look back, not as you go through it. Your new world is one of wistfulness. It may always be so. But there will eventually be a way to move forward. To feel like you are living your life again. However, it will always be punctuated with longing. This longing is particularly noticeable when something special happens in your life. You long to tell the person who you've lost. You long for their presence so that they can share the special day. You know as time goes on that they cannot be there. You have accepted it to a large degree. But that space of longing will always live on. Heartbreakingly, in your new reality and your new normal, you finally come to realise why they were laughing, you come to understand why the bin men continued to collect the rubbish and why the birds kept singing.

Absent Friends

As a teenager, a very good friend of mine lost her father to cancer. I remember the day well. I was at school when a nun came to our classroom to inform us that the girl's dad had died the night before. She was met with silence as a group of fourteen year olds tried, in vain perhaps, to digest such news. I recall having absolutely no frame of reference to truly understand what this might mean for my friend. Our worries of the day were as trivial as remembering all the ingredients for whatever dish we would cook for home economics or wondering if we would be unlucky enough to be picked to recite the passage we were to have learned for French. I was completely unable to relate to what she may have been feeling. As she never spoke of it, beyond the day of the funeral, I never spoke of it either. For years, in the silence of the morning I prayed for him. I prayed to God, to a spirit or to the hope of something greater than humanity. Every day I remembered him. Life moved on, the friendship drifted and I have not seen this girl in years. And yet, even to this day, I remember him. In all the years, I never told my friend. For we never spoke of it.

I never once thought it could happen to me. Perhaps you were the same, never conceiving that something like this could befall you. It would never be you who'd receive a call in the middle of the night, and in your dreamlike state hear a voice urging you to come to the hospital immediately. These things happen to other people. It would never be you who'd receive a knock at the door unstilling the quiet of night. This would not be your reality. Once that terrible threshold has been crossed, you cannot go back. The gap is too wide. The distance between your old life and new reality is too great to make a return journey. And the irony is that you'd never realise just how close to the edge you really are. We all hover there, never truly knowing, never fully appreciating, never thinking of the what ifs.

We start off life's journey in an innocent existence, a world of wonder. The world is a jewel just waiting to be explored. Danger, as yet, is an unknown concept. Babies sleep with their arms wide open, unaware of pain, danger or worry. They are totally trusting. That is until life touches them and the reality of a world in which hurt and pain do actually exist begins to dawn. Later on, when we sleep it is with arms wrapped tightly around us as if this may somehow protect us.

For so long, I lived in this safe place, never truly realising just how safe it was. For it is only when you experience the worst that you can look back and realise just how good life was, just how lucky you were. Of course, I knew people who died. Grandparents, aunts, uncles, cousins. In fact I had been to countless funerals and watched with sympathy as others fought to comprehend what had happened. They were on that terrible threshold, unaware of how utterly different their new reality would be and how they would never return to their old existence. I didn't know that at the time though. Naturally, I sympathised, sent a card, made a follow-up phone call after a few weeks and thought fondly of the dead. But that was it. It didn't stop my world in its tracks. I, personally, never knew the physical pain of grief until my parents died. I never knew that feeling of heartbreak, where it hurts so much that it feels you can't breathe. I had twenty-nine blissful years of not knowing it.

The people who were as I was before I lost my parents, I christened 'absent friends'. They didn't mean to be absent, of course. It wasn't their fault. Indeed many of them were well-intentioned, well-meaning and genuinely tried to offer support.

However, they had not crossed the threshold; they had not lost that precious somebody. So how could they truly understand?

I look back on my fourteen-year-old self and cannot understand how I failed to speak to my friend about the death of her father. How much did she miss him? Did she cry at night in the dark when no one could see? Did she worry that, having lost her father, she may lose her mother too? Would she ever feel normal again? Would her heart always be broken? Still I said nothing, mistakenly, simplistically believing that by not mentioning him, I would be sparing her further upset. I certainly was an absent friend.

Even so, even having been an absent friend myself, there were times when I blamed my own absent friends. Those who had not experienced such a loss had so little comprehension of how hollow their words sounded or how their reluctance to call wounded. They often said the wrong thing. They failed to remember anniversaries. This in particular I struggled with. When a date was forever marked in my heart, I failed to understand how those close to me could not remember it. But on reflection, who could blame them? For them it was still happening to that elusive 'someone else'. How could they know the right thing to do, to say? How I envied them in ways, hoping in vain to go back to that reality. And perhaps that was a large part of the problem. I saw in them what I used to be and longed to go back.

For every absent friend, fortunately I had truly present friends, for death is indiscriminate and knocks at many doors. As the absent friends may have unintentionally caused annoyance and exasperation, the present friends soothed and listened, calmed and cried with me. I took great comfort from those who had experienced similar loss. They had the wounds to prove it, and although their route was different, their journey was the same.

The guilt, anger, pain, depression, disbelief, shock and devastation had all been felt to some degree with varying stops in harrowing places.

There are exceptions of course. Not everyone who has lost a loved one was able to help me, able to fully understand. There are many reasons for this. Most importantly, grief is individual and unique. It has to be because no two deaths are the same, and even in the case of the same death, different loved ones will react in completely different ways. Every relationship is different. Therefore every loss is different. Also for some, their experience of loss was too far removed from mine; their reaction to the loss was unique to them or perhaps they were just at a completely different stage to me. They may well have had nothing left to give. There are no hard and fast rules with grief. Likewise, it is true to say that there are people in my life who, though having not experienced bereavement, were able to offer a genuine listening ear.

You may well find that it is difficult to share with friends who have had no experience of what you are going through. You may feel that they don't fully understand your innermost emotions. If this is the case, then give yourself some space from these people. You need to be in the most supportive environment where you can begin to heal.

Remember that the heart of an absent friend may well be full of support and love for you even if they are unaware of how to express this. You may even be fortunate to know some people who have not been bereaved, but, in spite of that, can be both understanding and supportive. Empathy can breach the gap between those who have experienced loss and those who have not.

The important thing is to listen to yourself, and if you are not comfortable or at ease in the presence of some friends, then gently excuse yourself. You may go to those who have experienced even the most devastating of losses and find them unable to support you. Everyone's journey through grief is different. Even within your family, you may be struggling with the discovery that no two people will grieve in the same way. Surround yourself with those who can best support you and meet your needs as they change on your journey through grief. One of the best things you can do is share the many complicated emotions associated with grief that, by necessity, must be explored.

A Journey We All Must Take

I never knew that I was capable of such love. When his dark blue eyes looked into mine, everything else faded away and it was just me and him. I thought my heart would burst. I had waited so long for this moment and it was worth every second. I would have waited forever for this. He was beautiful. He was little. He was utterly helpless but oh so perfect. And he was mine. As I held my beautiful baby boy for the first time and breathed in his wonderful scent, I vowed to protect him. To be by his side always. I would be his shield and his shelter. As I leaned over him to gently kiss his forehead, I couldn't believe how lucky I was to be blessed with a child.

Death now scares me. In fact, some days death terrifies me because I am truly aware of its power and destruction. It haunts me, taunting me about who will be next to be taken from my world. Once I had experienced the loss of a loved one, I came to a terrifying reality. I had crossed the threshold of loss and I finally realised that death does happen. I lived in a world in which people do actually die. A world from which people I love can disappear.

I had lost an innocence that I would have paid anything to retrieve. I would love to live in a carefree reality where the worries and stresses of the day were trivial. Instead, I now became concerned about the death of those around me, for I knew now, with certainty, that they too would die. It is a very frightening thought. It became a constant ache and knot of anxiety. I became weighed down with mortality. I knew the sobering truth that my loved ones can, but more importantly, will die. As I looked back, I was jealous of my old reality. Perhaps I was naïve, but life was simpler. And all of a sudden it had all changed and I was unable to bear the thought of attending so many funerals that I know will definitely happen.

Sometimes the fear lies buried in my subconscious, but when it awakens, I feel such a drop in the pit of my stomach as I am reminded yet again what it would be like to have such love taken away. Other times it is to the forefront of my mind and I wonder how I will cope when something does happen. Unfortunately, it is no longer an *if*. It is now a *when*. In a way it is like living with a ticking time bomb. I can become lost in it and it can be utterly depressing. On reflection, even though I didn't live a reckless life, I lived as though I and my loved ones were immortal. But now I am aware in the most intimate way of the mortal nature of our lives.

My new reality also led me to know, with certainty, that I too would die. It is perhaps something that people believe they already know. But after the death of a loved one, the knowledge is so much deeper. I found that in the beginning this manifested itself for me in a lack of drive. I strived to see the point to anything. I struggled with trying my best. At the close of the day, we will all die, so I wondered what the point was. Why bother? Why did it matter when in reality life was so short and could be taken away from us at any moment? Why put so much effort and care into life when really we were all on the road to the end? It paralysed me. It stopped me from making an effort and living life to the full.

When I became a mother, the worry intensified. My own mortality brought with it a new concern as I wondered how my son would cope without me. It led me to consider my own mother and if she had experienced similar feelings around her own mortality and that of her children. How many times did she lovingly pull the blankets over me? How long did she spend watching over me as I slept, hoping with all the love in her heart that life would be kind to me? And when I was ill, how she must have worried. When I was late home on a dark and lonely night, did she imagine the worst? It was only now that I realised she and I probably shared the same worries and fears. The wonderful feeling of joy when my son was born was in conflict with the fear of being parted from him.

When, with the passage of time, the shock lessened somewhat, I began to view the impact of mortality in a more constructive light. While I continue to struggle with the knowledge of my own impending death whenever that may be, it now serves as a reminder of the preciousness of life. It exhorts me to live, to make my mark and to truly enjoy life. Regarding the mortality of my friends and loved ones, I was paralysed with fear for a long time. Worry was my daily companion and it was difficult to let go. While I still worry about my loved ones, this worry now serves to prompt me to express my love for them and to create memories. It encourages me to communicate more and to share the most precious gift of all with them – time.

Dwelling on the thought of losing another precious loved one from your life is a totally normal response following a bereavement. Even your own death may preoccupy your thoughts. This can result in an awful, crippling fear. You may wonder and worry about when you will die, how you will die and if it will be painful. There is no magic solution to rid your mind of these thoughts. They need to be expressed in whatever way you feel able to do so. Our own death is inevitable and part of the circle of life. You now know this with certainty. What you also know is that this is outside of your control. You do not know how or when. Communicate your fears because worrying about your own death or that of a loved one, natural though it is, if left unchecked can result in a very unhealthy existence for you. Speaking about the fear of your own death or that of your loved ones will help. As you well know, death is a part of life. This knowledge brings with it understandable fear and anxiety. Turn that knowledge, however frightening, to your advantage. Live, really live and achieve all that your heart desires. Love and articulate that love as much as possible.

This has been the most difficult chapter for me to write. It forced me to confront something that lay beneath the surface. But more than that, it forced me to confront my greatest fear since my parents' deaths. The fear of losing another precious loved one. It has, however, provided me with a great gift, affording me an opportunity to have that conversation that I never had with my parents. If you are worried, speak to your loved ones about their death. Try to get past the nervous laughter, the deflective jokes or the possible refusal to discuss it at all. Turn this into something positive for those other wonderful people in your life. See where the conversation leads you. You might discuss your loved ones' wishes, you might discuss your own. You might talk about what they believe happens when we die. You may discuss what their wish for you would be. These discussions may even reassure you about the loved one you have lost. It can prove to be so worthwhile on a number of levels. Take your fear and turn it into something you can treasure.

Is, Was, Are, Were

To me, hearing my parents being spoken of in the past tense was like hearing a foreign language. One so remote that it left me dazed and upset. I didn't want to hear of them in such a way, so out of the ordinary did it seem. Remember when ... She used always ... He was a good man ... They were wonderful ... She was a great one for ... Didn't he always love to ...

For so long your loved one is a part of your reality, your daily life. They belong to your present. To hear as early as the funeral, only a couple of days after they have been ripped from your life, everyone speaking of them in the past tense can be too much to bear. This was a difficult reality for me as people began to change how they spoke of my parents, referring to them in the past tense. I marvelled at how easy it was for them to speak of my parents in such a way. For a long time, I continued to speak of them in the present. It physically pained me to hear them spoken of in a way that I had never heard before. As they did so, it angered me, unjustifiably so perhaps, but it was nonetheless how I felt. I could not bear my mother and father being confined to the past and I refused to place them there. In retrospect, this was perhaps an extension of the disbelief I had been feeling from the beginning. Even though I thought disbelief had been cast aside, it persisted. It served to remind me once again that grief is illogical and takes its own course.

I spent much time delving into the past. It was nostalgic and wistful but it also involved painful longing and a desperate hope to go back. It represented a time when I had all I needed. Implicit in this, of course, is that the present no longer fulfilled me, as it did not contain what I wanted. When I heard someone speak of my parents in the past tense, it only served to make it real and this was the reason I struggled so much with it. They may have left, but it was not something I was ready to accept. It didn't matter to me what people thought, I was not ready to speak of what was very much still my present in the past tense. It felt that to do so would be a disservice to my parents' memory.

However, eventually and gradually I reluctantly used the past tense too. The transition was not without difficulty. I dreamed a lot those days. I dreamed of my parents, and as I consigned them to the past, I wondered did they protest. Did it mean I loved them less or that I was coping, finally accepting that they were gone? Now I too, like others, spoke in a language tinged with sadness. I struggled with this, wondering did it suggest that I had moved on. Still though there are days – months and even years on – when I catch myself speaking of them in the present. It is another conflict as my past and my present battle it out, each refusing to yield; eventually the present emerges victorious.

And indeed my parents are my past; born of them and born to them, they represent my beginning. At first, my every move, my every breath was watched by them. Growing and developing, they took a step back as I started to become who I now am. Significant milestones and celebrations took place with both of them by my side. They are no longer part of this world, but their influence lives on, still shaping me, meaning that they will always be part of my present. They are my future for I will now forever take a glimpse back before I look forward.

Do you hear yourself say 'is' when you mean 'was'? If so, say 'is' for as long as you need to. Let 'was' and the past tense come only when you are ready. Don't feel guilty, don't feel ashamed. Be your own master of time. Allow the past as much time as it needs to admit defeat. It is a huge step. It is a part of the acceptance journey and it may take years. Your loved one has been your present for so long. But now, all of a sudden, they have been removed from your day-to-day life. To truly acknowledge and understand this is emotionally gruelling. Tread gently, for the truth is much deeper. However much we hate to use the past tense when speaking of our loved one, however anomalous it seems, the reality is that they are your past, your present and your future, and always will be. A tense, a language does not change that. How you or others speak of them does not change anything. It is but another inconvenient practicality as the world moves once more before you are ready to move. Remember though: past, present and future, and it will always be so.

I Lost You, But You Lost Everything

What would you have done, if you knew? If you had known: that this morning's sunrise, as the darkness was once again dispelled, was the last one you would ever witness; that the conversation you had today enclosed the precious last words you would ever utter; that as you sat and ate one last delicious meal, made more special by the presence of family, it was to be the final time you would sit around that kitchen table as you had done thousands of times before; that as you danced the night away and the evening came to a reluctant end, it was to be the last time you would ever dance. What would you have done differently? And yet, perhaps, if you did know, you might have done everything exactly the same. You mightn't have changed a single thing.

I am not quite sure if I am the only one who has wondered this. But often I worry about what my mother has lost. While I have lost my mother and her life on this earth is over, I am sad about all the things she has loved and the life she lived, that for her is no more. As she lay dying in a hospital bed, the words of a poem I had studied as a teenager, and could not possibly fully understand then, came to mind. It was Dylan Thomas urging, pleading with his father not to go gently into the night of death, begging him to rage, to fight against the dying of the light. I, too, wanted my mother to fight. I wanted her to fight for the life she loved so much, for the things in that life she was so passionate about. Unfortunately I discovered that for all the raging, the longing and the wanting to live there was nothing that could be done.

Faced with that reality, a huge part of my grief was for my mother's loss, for her loss of experiences. I couldn't get away from the fact that while I had lost my mother, my female presence, my guide and comforter, she had lost everything – her children, her grandchildren, her passions and habits of sixty-three years. What a change, what a loss for her. And even though she was no longer here, I worried for her. How would she cope? While I had believed in an afterlife and had faith before my parents had died, it was incredibly difficult to imagine where they might be. I wondered where my mother was and if she was okay. It was the simple things that bothered me – was she happy, warm, safe? I worried for such a long time about her that it was difficult to get over my deep sadness at her own loss.

It was precisely because I didn't know where my mother was that I wondered if she no longer experienced all the wonderful things that made her existence so joyful. How I hoped that she would in fact be capable of missing them. Because if she was able to miss all the wonderful parts of life then, even though she would be in a different reality, her existence at some level would continue, and that was what I longed for more than anything.

Nevertheless, I continued to grieve on her behalf for all the experiences that, for her, were perhaps no more. I cried that she would never again see the sun set on a summer's evening. She would never smell melting tar on the rare hot summer days. She would never again look at sweet pea, reach over, pluck some and gently arrange them in a bunch, closing her eyes and breathing in their wonderful scent. I wondered would she miss the rain that watered and nourished her much loved flowers and shrubs. And if she somehow knew in advance of the loss of all these wonderful parts of her life, would she too have cried in the knowledge that she never again would cry or laugh?

It was some months after her death that I began to wonder if my mother's awareness continued. Does she miss walking barefoot on a sandy seashore on a summer's day? Is her existence less beautiful for the absence of a piece of haunting music that would have touched her soul? Or can it still touch her soul? Does she miss her garden, the wonder of nature, of tending lovingly to flowers, shrubs and trees? Does she miss the feel of soil as it gently falls through her fingers? What about the beauty as her hard work finally comes to fruition? Or has she simply moved on to an entirely different existence with its own realities and experiences? Or is it the best of both worlds?

Does she long for the smell of roses on a fresh summer's day or do they waft right up to where she now resides? Does she miss sunlight lifting her heart and soul or is she so lifted that she has no need of sunlight? Does she think of her grandchildren that her arms simply ache to hold or does she busy herself watching over them, a guardian angel of sorts? Does she miss the simple pleasure of garden birds as they flutter and sing happily, delighted that someone has remembered to feed them on a frosty winter's day, or do they surround her now? Does she long for just one more cup of coffee and a chat or does she already know all the gossip, all the news and chatter of her loved ones? Does she wish for a hug from her loved ones or does she wrap us all in an embrace from above? Did she miss my wedding day or was she the one that, despite predictions of rain, made the sun shine?

Does she miss that smile and nod of recognition – you know, the one when you are happily surprised to see someone you know, not expecting them to be there too. But maybe she already has that where she is. Maybe she spends her days catching up with people she hasn't seen in years, with laughter as the soundtrack to her new existence.

I didn't want this to be it for her. No more tomorrows, the last and final today. I wanted to show her more of the world from my perspective. There was so much more for her to do, to discover, so much more life to be lived. This should not be the end. The truth is, we won't know until our own final moment comes. We can guess, wonder and ponder, but to be honest all we can really do is hope. I hope against hope that wherever my mother is now her existence continues and it is one of peace, happiness and beauty. I hope it echoes all that was good and meaningful in her previous existence.

Do you ever wonder about your loved one? Do you worry about them? Do you ever spend a little longer examining that phrase and philosophy that is so often uttered of finally being 'at peace'? It is perfectly normal to think more about this. To wonder about their new reality and existence and to go on worrying about them, hoping that they are in fact at peace and free of pain. Why not reflect on your loved one's passions and joys, the things that lit up their face? Reflect on what it was they loved; the things that made them who they were. There are no definite answers but the unique legacy of your loved one remains. Their shadow can still be seen and their echo still heard.

Emotions Run Wild

I remember years ago, as a child, witnessing a powerful and fascinating scene from nature. I noticed a crow on the grass in my back garden, lying still, motionless. Suddenly there was a loud, raucous noise; I looked up and above me were hundreds of crows. Their sorrowful cries filled the sky. I can still hear their mournful calls. They swooped and flew over and over, soaring above the dead bird, their fallen friend, one of their own. They were so utterly certain in their grief that he was gone. How did they know? How did they know that they were never to see him again? I remember being so surprised and fascinated at the incident, and in a way privileged to have witnessed it. And now, I wonder if we were able to express our grief so openly would it make it easier to share that grief, to feel the emotion and express it, thereby processing our grief more readily. It is reminiscent of the keening that took place at Irish wakes years ago on the death of a loved one. The keening was like a deep lament in the form of an eerie wailing, its purpose to express and release that pain of missing, the pain of loss.

In Ireland particularly, we offer as a greeting 'How are you?' Many will agree that it is in fact not meant as a question on your general well-being but more as an alternative to 'Hello'. If you attempt to answer it in detail, you may find your companion has moved on and was never actually expecting you to answer the question. Very often I gave the standard 'fine' or 'grand', as I didn't really know if the person asking me wanted a truthful answer. It's a pity, really, as it is such a useful question if we can truthfully answer to a genuine listening ear. Sometimes I felt that the person posing the question would not know what to say. Perhaps they would be so shocked at my response, at how absolutely wretched I actually felt, that they would be unable to cope with my honesty. However, the reality is that I did not really know for sure. It was unfair to assume what they may or may not say; to predict how they would react when I was not even giving them the chance to respond. But more importantly, I was not being true to myself and answering thus did me no favours at all, as I denied how I was really feeling.

I decided to try to be honest. How was I? There were days of numbness when I felt absolutely nothing; when if I was paid to name an emotion I was feeling, I could not have done it. There simply was no emotion in me. These empty days could strike at any time. Sometimes I felt utterly removed from everything, as if my parents were now so far away that we were completely disconnected. Everyday things that would have brought great joy were now a source of nothingness. Instead I felt a deep emptiness. Meeting friends, making dinner, watching a movie, dancing, a beautiful sunny day could not remove this emptiness. In a way it was like being in a desert, where the barren landscape lets no respite. I was no longer in the moment because part of my mind was always in the past, and so I was unable to savour the present.

How was I? There were moments of absolute soul-destroying sorrow when I thought I would never, ever stop crying. There were occasions when all I felt was red-hot anger and I couldn't get past the injustice of what had happened. There were instances of pure hopelessness. There were times of despair when I wondered what the point of life was, times when I failed to see the point of living and being the best you can be when it was only going to end. There were the periods of regret and guilt. There were days when these emotions mingled and I was feeling some or none of them. Every day was different and I could never predict how I was feeling until I stopped and reflected on what today brought for me in this journey of grief.

A deep-seated emotion can be likened to a scar. A scar fades but its mark remains. The initial pain makes you cry out. Then it subsides until it becomes a nagging ache. Eventually, after years perhaps, it twinges every now and again. But the mark of what you have been through stays forever. You run your finger over it, feeling its rough edges and its ridges, and as you do so, you are brought back to that time, to that pain. You are returned to the initial shock of when it all began, never realising beyond the initial gasp of pain what a long, painful road was in fact ahead.

There were words that months and even years on were still capable of taking my breath away and shattering any emotional stability I thought I may have found. I am sure you know what I mean. For me, when I heard the words 'chest x-ray' or 'high-dependency unit', I was instantly thrust back to that heartbreaking time just before my mother died. They are the words that made me feel that I was back at the beginning of my grief. I never wanted to hear those words again. They immobilised me. You, too, probably have words that stop you in your tracks. There may be situations also where your loved one would have always been, that bring you to a complete standstill. Perhaps it is a family dinner, a special occasion or simply something you always did together. One of mine was when I saw my nephews, my parents' grandchildren, growing up. I worried that they would have no memory of my parents. Sometimes they surprise me though. Recently, my eldest nephew, who is seven, told me that when he grows up he will build a time machine so that we can have Papa and Gran back again. I worried that my parents would never touch their lives but I think I need not worry about that – their influence and their memory will always be part of them.

It is painful to acknowledge and be aware of your emotions. However, you need to be present to your emotions, otherwise it will be impossible to work through them. Ask yourself every day how you are feeling – take a little time to yourself to assess your emotions because they are not always apparent. Observe what your body is doing – are your muscles clenched, are you slumped down in your seat? Take the time to notice. When you have acknowledged how you are feeling, try to be true to the emotion. If someone asks you how you are, attempt to tell them instead of saying for the seventh day running that you are grand. If this is too difficult, choose a close friend or relation who genuinely cares and wants to know how you really feel, and confide in them. You may bury your emotions from the world but you cannot hide them from yourself. Eventually they will come out. Once you acknowledge them, you can start to deal with them. Perhaps if we could be more open and true to these feelings when we lose a loved one, we would be able to process this huge range of emotions more honestly.

THE STORY

For a long time, I became obsessed with the search for a sign from you. A sign that you were nearby, some signal of your continuing existence. For some time, there was nothing. Perhaps the pain I felt at your passing meant that I could sense nothing else. Then a number of coincidences took place that probably wouldn't mean much to others. But it meant that I started to see you reflected in all kinds of places. I heard such a beautiful echo of you one day while out clothes shopping, of all things. Two wonderful old ladies stood discussing the merits and demerits of their possible purchases. 'I know I am a granny,' one said, 'but I don't want to look like a granny.' I went to speak to them. They reminded me of you so much and I ended up having a wonderful chat with these two complete strangers. I see traces of you everywhere and I hope with all my heart that your story is not at an end.

Everyone has a story. It weaves its own path in and around the events before, during and after a loved one's death. It is littered with sadness, tears and despair but it may well be scattered with happiness and funny moments that make it a very precious tale. It has characters, significant and insignificant. Doctors and nurses play their part too. It is a story of death though, so there may well be no heroes. The story is vitally important. Although for some, they may never retell that story as it might simply be too painful or too personal, for others, it's impossible to count the number of times that the story must be retold, even if just to themselves as they struggle to comprehend it. As you tell your story, you may well wonder if it really happened to you. You'll question how you managed to hold everything together and how you came out the other side.

My story is essentially broken into three parts. The story began, though I did not know it at the time, with my father's diagnosis of Alzheimer's. Here, unknown to me, was the beginning of his end – the start of his death story. It was only in retrospect that this became apparent: the gradual loss of memory, the lack of recognition, and, ultimately, the body pursuing the mind in being unable to continue and eventually surrendering. The second part of my story included the actual deaths of both my parents, just days apart. This was probably the most obscure part of the story – that part that, when I looked back, I questioned if I was there for at all. I wondered how I got through it, how I held conversations or drove to and from the hospital. Afterwards I marvelled at how, in the middle of the chaos, the normal, everyday acts were somehow also completed. This part of the story contained the precious details of the final moments of life. The third part of the story was probably the hardest. It involved those hours and days following the deaths as the reality sunk in. It possessed such a range of emotions that I did not know I was capable of feeling in such a short space of time. This third and final part of the story continues for me still.

When a baby is born into a family, we seek every little detail of that baby's birth. We not only hold the date of birth precious, but we also want to know the exact time to the minute. We want to know their weight, length, the colour of their hair. In fact there is a whole story built around how they were born, when labour started, and finally, the moment everyone was waiting for, the moment labour ended and that much longed-for little person's life began. We wonder did they cry straight away? Who was there to witness such a momentous event? It is a story proudly conveyed to family, friends and neighbours over and over again. Indeed it is a story that the little baby itself gets to know as they grow up;

recognising what an important part the beginning has to play in the rest of their life.

Death is similar. Every single detail, no matter how small, is greatly significant. Was the person conscious just before they took their last breath? Were they alone or surrounded by loved ones? Was the death sudden and unexpected or was it foretold by medical staff? Was there a quiet acceptance of the death or was there a fight to overcome the inevitable? On what date did they take their last breath? At what time did your loved one's life on this earth cease? You want to note every particular. You would record it but there really is no need, as each detail of that death story will be imprinted on your brain and in your heart forever.

It is important to dwell on the death story, at least initially. As you do so, you allow it to sink in. You are enabled to actually process the dreadful events that have unfolded. Eventually you will find that there comes a time when you no longer need to go over it again and again. It has become a part of you. The death story of your loved one becomes a part of your own story, so significant an event is it. It is, however, not the whole story. Eventually you will process it sufficiently that it won't occupy your every thought. Instead you will realise that your loved one is bigger than their death story. Just as there is more to a baby's life and story than the events surrounding their birth, your loved one's story encompasses their birth, their death, but more importantly the life they have lived in between.

That story too needs to be shared: the memories, exploits and passions of your loved one are just as important. Their hopes and dreams, greatest achievements and even their failures are all significant. Write them. Tell them. Dream of them. Share them.

Think of them often, especially if the death story threatens to take over. Keep the whole story alive. Remind yourself that because the inevitable – death – has actually happened, this does not make their story a sad one. Just like life, it is full of happiness, sadness, humour, sorrow, love and the myriad emotions that we can feel. And it is a story worth telling. Otherwise, why did you love so much in the first place?

JEALOUSY

I have struggled with jealousy. Every woman that lived to be more than sixty-three years old became a source of fascination for me, a source of wonder, of what-ifs, and of a sense of deep unfairness. It seemed as if life taunted me. As I turned every corner I saw a reflection of me with my mother. I railed at the injustice of it all. And the randomness of it. Why were these women allowed to go on, to continue living when my mother's life was cut short? I would have been grateful for one more year, yet I witnessed others living their lives as if they had no knowledge of its preciousness. I struggled to listen in silence as I heard daughters give out about their mothers. A lump formed in my throat as I watched mothers and daughters of all ages enjoy each other's company – something I could never again do.

During my journey through grief, jealousy has been an incredibly difficult emotion for me to deal with. The reason was twofold. Firstly this emotion really surprised me. It wasn't something I was expecting to feel. On reflection, I would have expected the anger, the regret, the pain, the longing. But jealousy startled me. Secondly, it is quite an ugly emotion to deal with. It is not a nice feeling. This has made it more difficult to deal with it especially because it makes it harder to share with others. Nonetheless, it was part of my journey and therefore it became necessary to stop a while and dwell on the emotion.

I can remember a particular day when I was sitting having a quiet coffee when two women sat beside me. I was drawn to them and tuned in to their conversation as I wondered if they were mother and daughter. It soon became apparent that they were. Much silence punctuated their stilted conversation. I realised with shock that not alone was I jealous, I was also angry. I was jealous that they still had each other, and angry at how they seemed to be wasting it. This is what I mean about jealousy being such a difficult and convoluted emotion. In truth, I had no insight into these two women, their relationship or emotional well-being. However justified I might be in feeling jealous, I could not understand why I would feel angry towards two women of whom I knew nothing.

When I saw new mothers watching over their precious newborns, I could not tear my eyes away. I wondered did my mother watch over me similarly, with such love lighting her face. I observed as mothers gave grown-up daughters support and love as they became mothers for the first time and I knew with cruel certainty that this was no longer in my future. I looked on as twelve year olds shopped for their first disco outfit with their mothers and my eyes misted over as I remembered doing the same. I saw mothers with tear-filled eyes bring their children to school for the first time and I longed to remember my own first day. I observed mothers shopping with their daughters for their wedding dress and I wished my mother could have shared that precious experience with me. I was jealous, resentful and angry. For months, every funeral I attended I spent working out how much older the deceased had been than my mother. And if my mother lived to be that age, how many more days we would have had together. And I was jealous.

This jealousy was illogical; however, grief will take away perspective. It was not a nice feeling. It certainly wasn't pretty. It was, however, part of it. Eventually I realised that I had to stop. I had to free myself of these unhealthy negative feelings. Comparisons are never useful – there will always be people better off and worse off when we make comparisons. It was certainly true for me. There are people who lost their parents when they were much younger than I was. There are others who never knew their parents at all. And, of course, there are people whose parents lived right into old age until they became great-grandparents. There is always better and worse. Making these comparisons doesn't help and I really feared that I would become bitter if I continued.

Eventually I dealt with the jealousy, but not without first allowing myself to feel it in all its power. I let myself ask why a thousand times until I didn't need to ask why again. Eventually, unimaginable as it seemed before, why became unimportant. No matter what answer I obtained, it would not change my reality. I allowed myself to say how unfair it was over and over and there came a time when I didn't need to say it anymore.

Instead, when I saw a mother organising a birthday party for her child, it afforded me an opportunity to remember the childhood birthday parties I enjoyed. When I saw a mother sit and have coffee with her daughter, it opened up wonderful memories of the many times we simply sat and shared our day over coffee and cake. If I noticed a mother and daughter on holiday together, it presented me with such wonderful recollections of shared holidays. Something negative had been turned into a positive and I learned to react in this way when I witnessed scenes that reminded me of my mother. Eventually, as I strolled around town or went to the cinema or walked in a park, I reminisced freely and a host of wonderful recollections came to mind as the feelings of jealousy melted away.

The way I see it now, with some perspective, is this: if I had another year, five years or even ten years, the pain and loss would be the same. Perhaps the more time I had with my parents, the harder it would be? I will never know. We think we have forever. But there are no forevers, and no matter when the time comes, we are unprepared, unwilling to let go. I have come to realise that if you love someone, you will never be ready to say goodbye.

It may be some relief to acknowledge that jealousy could be a part of your journey. While it can be a deeply unpleasant emotion to deal with, it is normal to ask 'Why me?', to wonder why such a tragedy has befallen you and not someone else. It is difficult to observe the rest of the world as they continue their lives unaffected. It reminds you all the more of what you have lost. Recognise what you have lost, name all the feelings associated with the loss. Acknowledge the fact that it happened to you and, if you can, release the negative feelings to make way for the joy that remembrance can bring.

THE GREATEST DAY

It's your birthday today and I want to honour you in some small way. Just you and me. Just something only the two of us would do. I go to your graveside, and as I plant flowers of the deepest hues, I talk to you. I tell you about my day and how only thoughts of you have permeated it. Just before I leave, I turn to look at your grave once more and notice that since I have been here last, the pansies that I planted over a year ago have taken off, their seeds spread by the wind, and now they are growing on the verge of your grave, and as I look I see they have spread to the next grave and the next and the next. I realise that your spirit lives on. I realise that you will never truly be gone.

All the special days in my life – the days that would have had meaning for me and my parents – are a struggle. On days such as these, I grapple with their absence as it is felt more strongly. Connected to this is a fear I have. It is a fear of change – of changing anything in my reality that my parents had knowledge of. I fear I will never again change jobs, move house, do anything different. I want my life to remain as it always was. If I change even the smallest detail, am I not betraying something? How can I make new memories, have new experiences when my parents are no longer part of it? I want to stay as I always have been so that they know where I am and what I am doing. In doing so, they are always part of my memories.

A really difficult experience for me was when I had to change my car. I remember buying that car, my first car, with my brother, present for his mechanical expertise, and my mother, simply because I could not imagine making such a purchase without her. We got a great deal and that car never let me down in six years.

As we drove in it together, memories of my mother driving us as children came flooding back. I remember being surprised at the role reversal as now every time we went anywhere together, I would drive. That car was full of happy memories for me, like one evening when we decided to drive an hour and a half to the seaside town we holidayed in every summer as a family, simply to play bingo. That was also the night, the only one I can remember, when we actually won money. I remember her excitement and I remember thinking how easy it was to make her happy. A few months after she died, I could have sworn she was sitting beside me as I drove. She had sat beside me so many times before, it seemed as if she was still there. So eventually when I had to change my car, I was heartbroken and all the grief and pain was reawakened.

I can place my parents in my house for dinner, for endless cups of tea, for random drop-ins, for marathon sessions in the garden, for hours and hours and memories and memories. I can see the chair in which my mother sat, the bed in which she slept. My parents simply have a place here. If I move, where will my memories of them be in a new house? I remember showing my mother around the small rural school in which I teach. She was enchanted, taking in every detail, finally able to picture me at work. Following the visit, she often asked me specific questions about how I do certain things in the classroom. On reflection, it was clear that she pictured me at work and this sparked off many questions for her. I want my parents to be able to imagine me as I always have been. That is who I feel I need to be now, the daughter they knew. I fear change. How can I ever change?

Whenever something special happens in my life, I am searching for them. I lose them all over again every time something important takes place. On days such as those, my greatest longing is to have them back again by my side where they should be. On the happy days, I am even more aware of their absence as I search for what it is that is causing such a hole of sadness in my heart. I do not have to search very long or very hard. Christmas Day, your own birthday, your loved one's birthday, Mother's Day, Father's Day, the birth of a baby: such happy days still, but tinged with longing and sadness. In the beginning, at times when I couldn't deal with these days, I largely ignored them. I wanted to stay in bed and sleep the day away. As time went on, I learnt to acknowledge my parents on these difficult days.

One of the hardest days since my parents died was my wedding day. Despite advice to the contrary, I walked up the aisle alone – the aisle down which my parents had taken their final journey. It was symbolic. No one could possibly take the place of my parents, who were perhaps at that very moment walking by my side anyway. My husband met me halfway. My parents had accompanied me thus far in my life and even though I wished they had stayed longer, it was now my husband who would accompany me on the rest of life's journey. The day was a mixture of emotion. It was so important to remember my parents on that day and I did so in a number of ways. The start of our wedding ceremony was the lighting of a memorial candle for them. Their photos were displayed prominently. I discussed my parents with our guests and received some lovely memories in return. I was grateful and it helped enormously that my parents both knew my husband, and my mother, in particular, was extremely close to him. The day was beautiful but bittersweet. I have come to realise that these days will forever be bittersweet. Time will never dull that.

It can be very difficult to get through a whole Christmas day. Christmas is such a personal time, personal to families in that each has their own particular rituals and no other family's day is exactly the same. Mine now starts with a very early morning visit to the grave. I feel I wouldn't be able to do much without first doing that. Often on those crisp winter days I am caught out with the sheer physical beauty of the day, which juxtaposes with the sadness in my heart. I go to the grave to say hello, I go to say happy Christmas, to say I miss them. I go because it is important that they know that on special days I haven't forgotten them. Rather, I miss them all the more.

Mother's Day and Father's Day are two days I could happily rip from the calendar and ignore completely. The first of these days after my parents died was extremely difficult. There are the people who mean well but say the wrong thing. One person pointed out 'Sunday is Mother's Day' and then a few seconds later, realising what this might mean for me, mumbled her apology and left. I know well that these people mean no harm. But sometimes in my own pain and grief, it is difficult to be around people during these times. The memories are ever present – of school days making cards, of flowers bought and family dinners together. Instead, now, on these days, I slip quietly to my parents' graveside for five minutes before continuing on with my day.

There are many special days for you too, I am sure. There are the days that affect everyone – Christmas, celebratory occasions where absences are noted. But also there are the days that only you will remember, only you will notice. These are difficult days. It can be hard to know where to go and what to do on days such as these. Eventually and over time, you will come to realise the difficult but nonetheless true reality of where it is that memories actually reside. It has been difficult to accept but memories are not buried in bricks and mortar, not in a house, a building, even a particular way of life. Instead memories are buried in hearts and minds, waiting to be rediscovered. It doesn't matter what you change in your life – your home, your job, your car – the memories will still be present. As for the happy days, the special occasions, you can get through these days, forever tinged with sadness but still a necessary part of life. And if you wonder what your loved one would have thought, you don't really have to think too hard, for they would want you to enjoy days such as these as best you can. They know and you know they will never be forgotten.

THE SAGE ADVICE OF OTHERS

What will I say to the one who has lost their lover, their friend, their mother, husband, wife, son, daughter? What will I say to the one who has lost everything? What words can I utter to my friend who now resides in grief, whose eyes fill with sadness, whose heart is broken? What can I say to such devastation? I know. Firstly, I will say nothing. I won't speak. First of all, I will listen.

There are too many sayings, I think. Too many sayings that have been handed down and are uttered over and over again. I wonder has the perceived wisdom ever been truly examined. These are the stalwart phrases that are used when nothing else will suffice. These are the phrases that you have heard over and over again, and perhaps you yourself have even pronounced the same words, thinking that you are helping. Now in your new reality, you realise that perhaps the words did not help. In fact you wonder why people keep repeating them.

'At least they are together now.' For me, this was quite a difficult phrase to hear and one I struggled with. I presume that because it is unusual for a husband and wife to die so close together, this was the reason people repeated these words to me. It was, from my perspective, not the most helpful thing to say, because this was the most difficult aspect for me – the fact they had both been taken from me together. I did not want my parents to be together in some nebulous and vague 'better place'. I wanted them here with me or, at the very least, I wanted one of them to remain with me and help me make sense of what had happened. Why the two of them had been taken together was quite beyond me and failed to offer me any vestige of comfort. These phrases were often coupled with 'at least they are not suffering now'. For me, this is a difficult one. It may offer comfort if perhaps your loved one suffered before death. But it is also somewhat hollow and difficult to prove or to believe.

'Time is a great healer.' This is another oft-used phrase. It does serve to fill the silence and may even be uttered by someone who truly believes it. However, it did not comfort me as was intended. Time does bring some level of acceptance as you process your loss. As every month goes by, your body and mind comes to some slow acceptance of the reality that your loved one is not coming back. However, time alone fails to heal; it simply allows the reality to sink in. Acceptance is a strange concept which is definitely helped along by time but it does not necessarily move in a linear fashion. There are points in your journey when you accept your loved one's death and other times when you still cannot believe it to be true. Two and a half years after my mother's death, I awoke having dreamt of her, only to do a check in my head and believe for a moment with relief that, yes, she was still alive. Even though time does aid acceptance, telling someone a matter of days following a death that it is a great healer may not be particularly helpful.

'I am sorry for your troubles.' This is a common phrase heard at funerals. It is usually a genuine expression of sympathy by family and friends. But sometimes the phrase can be used as simply something to say to fill in what can be an awkward silence. Another phrase used a lot at funerals to describe your loved one is 'the remains'. This I struggled with somewhat. The remains of the dead – that which is left. It generally meant your loved one's body. But when your loved one has died, what is, in fact, left? I struggled with the concept because, to me, there were no remains, for what constituted my loved one was gone. However, on reflection, when we examine exactly what is left, there is a lot more. I came to realise that there remains a lifetime of memories, there are children and loved ones left, there are influences above and beyond what you might have thought, there are ripples as your loved one's good deeds continue to have effect. In fact, when you examine it, what remains is in fact very significant.

'I don't know what to say.' This phrase, coupled with, 'there are no words', was to me probably the most honest of all words that can be spoken on the death of a loved one. It contains a simple truth and at the same time recognises the devastation that has occurred in your life. There are no words to explain this huge loss. There are no words to comfort when all the comfort you want is for this not to have happened. I appreciated the people who were honest enough to say this to me. Another more helpful phrase was 'How are you feeling?', so long as it was proffered with a true desire to listen to the answer and not for mirrored clichés from me such as 'You know yourself' or 'I'm surviving.'

'Has it really been two years?' I got asked this a number of times and it reminded me of the relativity of time. For me, it certainly had been two years and I had felt every day of it.

Advice was also offered though not always sought. For example, everyone had an opinion on when I should return to work. I was advised to go back to a routine as soon as possible. Those offering the advice did so with a good heart but did not understand the enormity of this decision for me. In the end, I stayed off work for two months as this was the time that I needed. Even then, I struggled with what that might mean – did it mean that now I was back at work I was okay, better, back to normal? Part of my routine had always been to call at my mother's house on the way home from work; I struggled to know what to do with that time now.

People offer platitudes because often they think that it is all they have to offer. Unable to articulate what we really want to say, we are afraid of the emotion and so instead use the time-honoured phrases that may have little else to their credit except that they are something people have always said. Remember, if the words offend or fail to comfort, search a little deeper for the meaning behind them. People's intentions are what counts. Your friends, family and those around you are essentially good and mean well. It is certainly not their intention to cause further hurt or sorrow.

What is important is that you listen to yourself and your body and make decisions for yourself accordingly. It's also important that you have someone in your life with whom you can share the deepest, darkest emotions of your grief. This may well be a counsellor: someone trained in bereavement and able to offer you the support you need. It may be a loved one who is willing to offer an unbiased and open ear.

Unanswered Questions

There is a tree in my front garden that garners much interest from visitors. Although I have a keen interest in gardening, I don't know what type of tree it is. However, it is shaped like an umbrella. Its branches reach to the ground, ignoring all natural instincts to the contrary to reach to the light. My mother shaped this into an umbrella tree and I don't remember how or exactly what she did to achieve this. All I remember is her joy on inspecting the tree and declaring that she would turn it into what it is now. It is just as beautiful in spring, with the beginnings of its rich green foliage, as in winter, when its bare branches stretch down towards the ground. I wish I could ask my mother how she did it, how she knew what to do, to teach me too. But now and forever more, it is too late.

There are so many questions that I wish I had asked. Too many, in fact. As my journey through life continues, and I experience more of life, the number of questions simply increases. I move on to different life stages and I encounter new events and long to ask so many different questions. I don't know why I didn't ask before. Why didn't I realise that life is not forever, that my parents would not always be here? How utterly naïve of me not to realise that death is a part of life. Now when it is too late, I berate myself for all those things I long to know but never asked.

I wonder about my parents' wedding. On that special morning on the first day of January, were they nervous, excited or a mixture of both? Why did they choose that day to get married – was there some significance for them attached to the first day of the new year? Did it perhaps symbolise the first day of their new life together? What was their favourite part of the day? Who helped my mother to choose her dress?

When they found out they were to be parents, how did they feel? What was it like for my mother to be pregnant? Did she suffer from morning sickness? On becoming parents, were they beyond excitement? Nervous? Fearful? Happy? Did they wonder what the future might hold? There are a multitude of questions that no one else can answer for me. Sometimes, questions occur at random times as I wind my way through a life that has been altered forever. It may be advice that I seek about a specific task I'm engaged in. It may be a bigger, more life-changing decision, and I wonder what counsel my parents would have provided.

I can, of course, ask other people who knew my parents. I can ask family members, those who knew them long before I was born. When I do so, on the one hand I am excited and hang on every new detail I find out about them. Everything I didn't know is a source of excitement and I feel as if I have them back for the briefest of moments. On the other hand, though, these memories pale into insignificance and are hollow as if all I am hearing is an echo of my parents. My longing to hear the answers from their own mouths is overwhelming.

I wonder what, if they knew that they were dying, they would have said to me. Would we have been able to accept it, get beyond the jokes and have a serious conversation about death? On the morning of my wedding day, what words of wisdom would they have offered? If they knew I was about to have a baby, what advice would they have given me?

About nine months after my mother died, I had to go for surgery. My mother had had the same surgery a few years earlier. At the time, I thought I had spoken to her about it and thought I knew all about it. But in reality, I knew very little and longed to compare our experiences. I wished I could ask her about it and I yearned for her to comfort me, to quiet my fears as I went on to the next unknown stage of the surgery.

Every wasted opportunity seemed to be highlighted as if pointing out all the things I never asked but should have. I wondered how to get a slip of hydrangea and plant it elsewhere. I had the one we took from my mother's garden. It was in full bloom, getting bigger every year and much admired. But how could I grow another one. I never asked my mother. Instead I was happy for her to do it for me.

Unfortunately, this is how it will always be. You will never be satisfied as there will always be questions as you continue to live your life. The honest answer to a myriad of questions is that you just don't know. For me, I don't know how my mother made the tree in my garden into an umbrella tree. The more people comment and ask about it, the more I want to know and wonder how I could not have asked. It only serves to increase my longing for another tomorrow. But I know in my heart of hearts that if I had a thousand tomorrows, it wouldn't be enough and the questions would still be there. You have to remind yourself of what you *do* know. You have to remind yourself of the wonderful thousands of yesterdays you have shared. You have to remember the many questions that you know the answers to without even thinking. You have to remember that they are plentiful and somehow content yourself with that huge part of your loved one that you are so familiar with.

Even if your loved one had lived forever, you would never have asked everything. Instead focus on all the things you do know. Ask others and increase your knowledge if you need to. Every little piece of information is like gold. But don't forget all the gold you already have – the thousands and thousands of nuggets that already belong to you.

WHEN THE LIGHTS GO OUT

Did lights shine out, guiding you home? Was there a tunnel, a transition, a journey of sorts before you reached your final destination? What was it like? Were you afraid? Afraid for yourself, not knowing, not understanding, unsure of where it was you were? Were you afraid for me? Did you glimpse how much pain was ahead and wonder would I cope? Did you miss me already?

The enormity of what I had lost took some time to fully resonate. For my entire life, there had been this bright light, but now the beacon of light and hope that burned for me had been quenched. For some time I didn't even consider a life after death or where my parents might be, as the struggle to comprehend their departure was all-consuming. With time, it became a burning question for me, one I almost became obsessed with. Is there a heaven, an afterlife, an alternate existence? Does life really continue after death?

What of my beacon of light and love? Has it gone out or does it go on burning? Does it burn on someplace that is not here? I am, it seems, one of a small minority of people who have never uttered the phrase 'rest in peace'. It seems that, for most, there is a great comfort to be had from the thought that your loved one is now at peace. From the moments my parents died and even now still, this philosophy completely fails to comfort me. I never wanted my parents to rest in peace. To me, it is quite a meaningless phrase if you consider it for a moment. Ironically, this is the one time that my parents have no need of rest. There is no longer a body weighing them down with its worries of life, its pains, aches, diseases and injuries. Perhaps ten years ago, I would have wished for them to have a rest, a brief respite from life, but not now when they have absolutely no need of it. Instead I wanted them to go on existing and living in whatever place they now found themselves. And even more than that, I wanted them to go on adventures together, to have an amazing afterlife existence, not simply to rest. If I am being completely honest, the thought of them resting in peace forever scares me because I don't know what that means for the reality of an afterlife.

My day job involves teaching four-to-eight-year-old boys and girls. Quite often the question of heaven and life after death comes up. Sometimes there is a trigger for this thought to enter a child's head. Perhaps a grandparent has died. Maybe the topic comes up as we are engaged in a religion lesson; other times there is no particular reason that I can discern. I answer this question a lot differently now since my parents have died. I used to explain that, yes, this is what the stories of Jesus tell us – that there is a heaven, an afterlife, and that is where we all hope to go when we die.

This quite possibly was the truth for me then; when I was innocent of these things, when I thought fondly of an uncle who had died and wondered where he might be. Wondered in curiosity, never in abject pain, devastation and worry. At that time, that childlike faith that I had no reason to question was as deep as it went for me. Now, following all that I have been through, when the children ask me, my answer is different. I tell them the truth, or what has become the truth for me. I still tell them that the Bible teaches us that there is a heaven, but I also explain that the only people who know for sure cannot come back and tell us. They seem to ponder this for a while and somewhat surprisingly it sits very well with them. I generally continue telling them that we will only know when we die. They nod their heads, accepting this idea. And I realise that there is much the children can teach me.

For me, there are a few ways of looking at the afterlife question. Firstly, the whole question can be presented in a logical manner, devoid of emotion. Arguments and points to support the existence of an afterlife, and equally to disprove its existence, can be made. For example, discussions may centre on the evidence of those who have had near-death experiences and, as a result, are now firmly of the belief that an afterlife does exist; while others will argue such experiences are the result of the body being starved of oxygen and do not prove the existence of an afterlife. I realise that this – the logical debating, presenting and arguing of facts – will never provide me with the answer I want. I will never know for sure about the existence or nonexistence of an afterlife by weighing up the arguments on both sides. I will not get that concrete, beyond-a-doubt proof that I so badly need.

The second way to look at it is purely on the basis of faith. This may well be a faith built on a lifelong practice of a particular religion. And, as I discovered, it could be a belief you hold all your life, and it is not until that moment when you lose someone special, that you realise you never really thought about the answer that your faith gave you. All my life, I had never questioned it much. I accepted it. I had no reason to question it at all. I always hoped it was true. But however I hoped and tried to cling to it, following my parents' deaths, it was not the thing that gave me comfort. On reflection, I was probably disappointed and a little surprised that my faith did not provide me with the answers I had hoped for. I still had my faith but it was now a faith that had been severely shaken.

What it came down to for me, after over two years of reflection on the topic, is quite difficult to put into words. It is not based on religion or any particular teaching. It is not based on any specific argument. There is no scientific proof, of course, no facts, no certainty. Instead it is based on instinct and a knowledge that is so deep it is part of my being. It is a feeling I have deep inside, a feeling I know beyond a doubt to be true. It is evident during my times of struggle, fear or pain – those times when I would have turned to my parents. I still do so and feel their reassurance. Sometimes it wells up inside and creates so much love and comfort for me knowing that my parents are somewhere, that they do indeed go on. Not resting in peace but actually existing, and knowing that, yes, some day I will meet them again. I don't need proof. It gives me comfort and utter absolute joy. Imagine seeing your loved one again. It takes my breath away – I suspect it always will. It is something so big that I can never fully understand. It is something I will always grapple with. I do, however, believe that my parents are somewhere above, some place beyond here. That they go on being. I know that I'll never again be truly alone. I'll never be totally frightened. My parents will always be there guiding, protecting, their light shining on. A relationship that was truly special is not ended by death.

You are the only person who knows what you believe. Perhaps you don't believe in an afterlife. You believe your loved one's life is truly over now and you keep their memory alive in all the ways you know how – by talking about them, displaying their photo, continuing to do the things you always did together. Or maybe it is your faith that tells you there is an afterlife and this is what you firmly believe to be the truth and perhaps what your loved one believed too. And this, possibly, gives you comfort on your grey and lonely days. Or maybe you are like me – you just know, you have a sense of your loved one's presence still in your life and you know in your heart and soul that they go on, that their existence continues. Whichever it happens to be, be persuaded in your own belief and don't change it for anyone, as this kind of truth – the truth that is yours – is intensely personal. No one can tell you, no one can make your mind up for you. It is your own creed, bigger than any one religion, a conviction that you hold because of your life's experiences and relationship with your loved one. Hold on to that belief, whatever it may be.

A New Reality

Sometimes I feel like I know a secret. I hug it close to myself. I know that you are there. It's not something I can explain but in the deepest part of my being I know it to be true. I finally realise that you watch over me and I feel your smile as the sun emerges from the clouds, warming me on a cool day. I feel your presence in my daily life. I feel your love. I feel your spirit hovering and watching over me. It is the most beautiful thing in my life and there are days when I feel like I am the luckiest person alive that I have you, forever, always right there watching over me.

For me the journey continues. It continues even though I have to travel it alone. I am changed forever. My companion is gone. But still I must carry on. Utterly changed though life may be, I know I have to keep going. On the bad days, that ache and longing is present. I continue in spite of it, knowing that it is what I must do. There are still days when the world is black and white, devoid of any trace of colour – when I fail to see the beauty of the reawakened spring or forget how truly blessed I am by the significant relationships in my life. There are days when good food and company fail to make an impression on the pain, when birdsong and beautiful music fail to penetrate the dark. There are still bright summer days with gardens of washing lines bursting with freshly washed clothes, days full of yellow and white daisies and heavy with the sweet smell of fresh-cut grass that are nonetheless tinged with sadness. There are days when something important happens in my life and I rush to tell my parents, only to realise again, with the deepest sorrow, that they are no longer here. On these days, I wonder how I can possibly cope with the recurring disappointment and I doubt that I have made any progress on this seemingly never-ending excursion through bereavement.

But there are also days when I feel my parents' spirits with me. When I finish a day of gardening, feeling the ache of hard work melt away, when I stand back to look at what I have cultivated and I know my mother is looking on too, admiring my hard work, proud of the skills she has passed on to me. When I feel frustrated and, without having to think, the words my mother would have used to dissolve the frustration come to mind as if she never truly left. There are times when I do alone what we would have done together and I smile as a memory of our shared experiences comes to mind. Childhood memories illuminate gloomy days. I know it will always be so. There is a lifetime of memories that will sustain me and even death cannot dim their radiance. The difficult, sad days prompt a renewed awareness of how much I have lost. If that which I had lost had not been so precious in the first place, then it would not still hurt so much. The happy, carefree days are a reminder too – they serve to remind me of what I had and in many ways still have because I am essentially so much of what my parents made me. Their deaths have also made me realise how precious this life really is. In ways, their deaths inspire me to do my absolute best, to make the most of this time, short though it is.

Now, over two years later, when I think of my father, it is always summer. He is sitting in the sun eating ice cream at a favourite seaside haunt. There is a certain tranquillity connected to my impression of him. When I think of my mother I think simply of yellow. I'm not quite sure why. Perhaps it was the vibrant yellow that clothed the kitchen walls of my childhood. Or the large bed of the most wonderful smelling yellow roses that covered the right-hand side of the driveway. Or it could simply be that when I call her to mind, she is always smiling. In every photo

I have and every memory in my head, her smile lights up her face. I can picture her in her garden, the sun she loved so much shining on her truly contented face. Yellow. It is a serene, relaxed colour, and this is how I picture her – finally at the end of her day, finding peace.

On reflection, my mother always had a problem with goodbyes. Regarding her family and particularly her children, she was a worrier. It was borne out of pure love. For her, the thought of any harm coming to her children would have been the absolute worst thing that could have befallen her. If any of us were leaving the house, she would always go to the door and throw holy water onto her departing child, her faith always strong. She would watch until we were out of sight, reluctant to let us go. She had a departing phrase for anyone that she would not see for some time. I remember her saying it to me when I was going to Africa for a few months. She would say, 'Don't say goodbye, say cheerio.' I like to think that this would be her philosophy for her own death also. I think we both believe it is not really a true goodbye, a final farewell, but more a matter of when we will meet again. And this has to be true because love never dies. It is too powerful an emotion to die on the death of a body. Love is stronger than that. It is so powerful that it truly lives on, overcoming death.

How would your loved one have said goodbye to you? What parts of them do you still hold on to and carry with you? Take the time to reflect on this to really understand how much of them you carry with you. You'll be surprised at how much they are still with you even though they are gone. Don't be surprised or feel in any way guilty at how much peace this can bring you. We know life must go on, however much we wish it didn't have to, but for you it is an altered life that will never be the same again. This is the new normal for you. Perspective taught me that this does not mean it is to be an entirely negative normal. The sadness at your loved one's passing will never leave you, but neither will all the happy memories, shared experiences and lessons you have learned. There is enough love for you to continue on. You will always wonder, hope, pray and miss. But you will also always love. You will continue to love your loved one until your own dying day, whether that is in ten years or sixty years. Years, the passage of time can never dull such a strong and powerful love. And afterwards, well, who knows? I like to think that it is so significant and powerful an emotion that in some place that is not here, that love goes on, only waiting to be reconnected. And when it is connected once more it will, after what seemed like such a long absence, be stronger than ever.